YOSEMITE
WILDFLOWER
TRAILS

Text and photographs
by
DANA C. MORGENSON

Published by
YOSEMITE NATURAL HISTORY ASSOCIATION
© 1975

CONTENTS

FOREWORD

The purpose of a National Park such as Yosemite is the preservation, in its natural state, of a great scenic area of national significance, together with all of its wildlife, be it plant or animal. Its objective is therefore to provide us with a great nature preserve of superlative character which we and our posterity may visit and enjoy. However, the privilege that we may have of its enjoyment carries with it a large degree of responsibility on the part of all of us to help maintain the natural conditions we should expect to find. The beauty that holds our eyes as we gaze over the wild landscape or examine more closely its detail is the result of ages-long interactions of an intricate complex of physical and biological forces. It has its fragile aspects, and this is notably the case as to the aggregations or scatterings of the particular kinds of flowering plants composing elements of the communities of vegetation. The flower-strewn areas and the flowers themselves, both of which we so admire, are easily disrupted by our thoughtless actions. All of us, by treading lightly and merely admiring, can leave but little if any trace of ever having passed that way.

In the following charming account our author introduces us to many of the wild-flowers of Yosemite National Park and enables us to know and thereby appreciate them more fully. He leads us to them through the seasons and along the trails he knows so well. His is a first-hand experience with them through many years of residence in the Park and travel on its trails. Moreover, he has had the good fortune of having been in long association with Mary Tresidder who had an abiding love for Yosemite's wild places and especially for its wildflowers. Her knowledge of the flowers was sound. I recall the several occasions when, at one or another of the Curry Company's High Sierra Camps, I would find by the door of the dining tent a newly-written, lengthy and accurate listing of, and interesting comments on, the flowers to be found in bloom in the immediate area during the week I merely happened to arrive. They were in Mary Tresidder's hand; she had fastened them there. And then, out on the trail, when perchance I found her together with a group of her old friends, her questions and comments on the flowers she had seen showed again her love and knowledge of them. Much of her love and knowledge of Yosemite's wildflowers she has passed on to our author.

Carl W. Sharsmith

5

PREFACE

Yosemite National Park, world-famous for its majestic granite cliffs and thundering waterfalls, is also a region of great appeal to the admirer and student of wildflowers. Many casual visitors are aware of only a few of the more showy species such as redbud, dogwood, azalea and lupine, but interested observation will disclose a fascinating array of flowering plants, seemingly endless in their variety of form, color and life habits. When one's interest and attention are drawn to this facet of Yosemite's splendor, it becomes a continuing source of delight and inspiration, increasingly so with each visit.

The great diversity in Yosemite's flora is chiefly a product of the pronounced altitudinal variations within the Park. On the western edge, near the El Portal entrance, the elevation is only 2,000 feet above sea level, within the Digger Pine-Chaparral Belt of the foothills. (Under the former Merriam system of life zone classification, this would be known as the Upper Sonoran Zone.) By contrast, the Sierra crest which marks the eastern boundary of the Park includes peaks reaching to heights of 12,000 to 13,000 feet, the so-called Alpine Zone. Between these two extremes are gradually increasing elevation zones which contain basins, canyons and mountain slopes, yielding wide contrasts in climate and soil conditions and thereby producing an amazing variety of plant forms.

One of the interesting concepts of plant occurrence in Yosemite is the sequence of wildflower blooming. This extremely pleasant aspect of the floral year is particularly associated in our minds with the season of springtime, when all the world of nature arouses itself from winter dormancy and begins its primary task of producing seeds and fruits—preceded, of course, by the beautiful phenomenon of multi-hued blossoms. Spring, according to the calendar, normally may be expected during the months of April and May, with the increasing warmth of June, July and August generally bringing an end to the period of bloom. Not so, however, in Yosemite National Park.

In this favored region, spring puts in its first appearance in early March (sometimes even in late February) with the earliest buttercups pushing through the greening turf of the Sierra foothills. As week follows week across the calendar, spring strolls in footsteps of beauty up the mountain slopes, stopping in a grassy meadow, then beside musical streams of icy melt-water, pausing to decorate a canyon's walls or to add vibrant colors to a lakeshore. As spring passes, each succeeding altitudinal zone of the Park comes alive with its own varieties of flowers. Finally, at the end of August, the pageant of springtime reaches its last act with the flowering of the gentians across the subalpine meadows while rock-fringe and alpine columbine bloom among the rocky fastnesses of the summit peaks. A blessed land is this, indeed, where one is privileged to enjoy six months of springtime, through the simple expedient of following the season vertically through the Park!

The purpose of this book is to provide a trail guide to these flowers of Yosemite, especially the ones most likely to attract attention. Within the confines of this small volume it was not possible to be more inclusive; over 1,500 classified flowering plants, shrubs and trees occur within Yosemite National Park. I will try to point out representative trails and roads where you may follow the ascending passage of spring. The book will attempt to list the most showy flowers in these areas and to suggest when and where they may be seen. Descriptions of the flowers have been phrased in nontechnical terms, emphasizing the salient characteristics of color, form, size and location which will enable the layman to make a ready identification. But for further use in studying these plants and their related taxonomic classifications, the scientific names have been included with the common names used in the Yosemite area.

Mary Curry Tresidder was one who knew and loved the wildflowers of Yosemite, with a deep sensitivity born of a lifetime spent in the Park. Though every other aspect of Yosemite was familiar to her as well—its trees, its birds, its waterfalls, its trails and its incredible scenery—the wildflowers remained her chief joy and constant inspiration. She understood their characteristics, knew where to find them and when to expect them, and felt ever at home among the flowered canyons and meadows of this part of the Sierra Nevada.

For many years she had considered writing a book on Yosemite wildflowers, hoping to communicate to others some of her own feeling for their unique charm, while assisting the interested beginner to learn more about them. Though she kept careful diaries and field records, the years slipped by and the book was never started. As she neared the end of her life, realizing she would never achieve this cherished goal personally, she decided to make provision in her will for the work to be accomplished.

This book is the direct result of her vision and generosity, reflecting a lifetime of interest in Yosemite wildflowers. Much of its material is based on her journals, diaries and articles she prepared occasionally for publication in newspapers and magazines. Additional field work has been done by the author along the trails and roads of the Park during many years of residence in Yosemite. I am deeply indebted to Dr. Carl Sharsmith, noted Yosemite Ranger-Naturalist, Emeritus Professor of Botany at San Jose State University, San Jose, California, and an outstanding authority on the flora of Yosemite, for checking the work for scientific accuracy.

Dana C. Morgenson

SIERRAN FOOTHILLS
AND THE APPROACHES
TO YOSEMITE

Visitors to Yosemite National Park who approach from the west—and this a large majority—travel through many miles of foothill country before arriving at their destination. Whether they use State Highway #41 from Fresno, #140 out of Merced or #120 via Oakdale and Groveland (the Big Oak Flat Road), such an approach will be enhanced by a pleasing variety of wildflowers in March, April and May.

As the first groundswells of the Sierra lift above the flatlands of the San Joaquin Valley, the wildflowers begin to appear. One of the showiest of these low-elevation plants is Tidy Tips (*Layia fremontii*), a very handsome member of the sunflower family. The foot-high, rather hairy, branching stems support flowers about two inches across. Orange-gold petals terminate in prominent white tips, giving the blossoms a distinctively elegant appearance. Tidy tips prefer the gently rolling grasslands of the lowest foothills, and are at their best in March and April. In March too, the open, sunny flats of these low foothills are blanketed by a tiny composite called Goldfields (*Baeria chrysostoma*). Only a few inches high, its uncounted numbers of individual yellow blooms make an impressive mass of color across the landscape.

Another brilliant tonal effect is created in this same area by a small white flower called Meadow Foam (*Limnanthes douglasii* var. *rosea*). It grows in great profusion around the borders of pools and seeps in the folds of the lowest hills, creating the illusion of frothy, white foam or isolated snow drifts, startling in the wide expanse of green grass. The individual flowers are attractively lined with pink veins across the petals and are on stems 4 to 10 inches high, but it is the total mass which produces its remembered beauty.

A type of flower commonly seen in this region is the genus known as brodiaea, of the lily family. In good wildflower years, at least five different species will be found

Meadow Foam in Sierra foothills

occurring in some quantity. Preferring the tall-grass hillsides in rather sunny locations, they grow on long slender stems, their flower heads a loose grouping of bell-like cups, usually blue or violet in color. One of the most common species, however, is called Golden Brodiaea *(Brodiaea lutea* var. *scabra)*, widely distributed through the foothills and flowering from March to early summer. Its color is an exception to the general rule for the others; as the name implies, it is a pale yellow, often closer to white, with a dark mid-vein on each of its six petals. As with all brodiaeas, its leaves are grass-like and grow from the base of the flower stalk.

Another memorable group of plants, also in the lily family, is the genus calochortus, familiarly called Mariposa lily. Some of the more common representatives of this genus develop large, open, bowl-shaped blossoms, in colors of white, yellow or lavender-pink, with vividly contrasting designs at the base of each petal. Growing on long, slender stems also, they are to be found from foothills to high mountains; we will find the white form of the Mariposa lily again in Yosemite Valley and later along the High Sierra Loop Trail. Perhaps the most exquisite of the calochortus (meaning, literally, "beautiful grass"—and the leaves *are* grass-like) is the Fairy Lantern or Globe Lily *(Calochortus albus)*. Its lantern-like blossoms, creamy white, hang pendent from the two-foot-high flower stalks, with a graceful quality of great appeal. Instantly, the similarity to Japanese lanterns is brought to mind. Look for these unusually beautiful flowers in shady, rather rocky locations and often, conveniently, in road cuts. They bloom in April and May.

One of the early bloomers, and one of the more colorful, is the charming little annual commonly called Baby-Blue-Eyes *(Nemophila menziesii)*. It can be found between 2,000 and 4,000 feet in grassy or brushy places, often forming pools of intense sky-blue where the blossoms crowd together. Sometimes these flowers are distributed broadly across grassy slopes, like fine stardust. Their 5-petaled flower cups, deep blue with white centers, are usually about an inch across and are borne on slightly hairy stems with compound leaves divided into many toothed segments. The deeply saturated blue blossom is easily seen as one drives the foothill roads, even though the flower stems are but 4 to 10 inches high.

In the same general altitude (1,300 to 5,000 feet) there often will be found great numbers of another striking blossom. Since it usually blooms in May, when much of the foothill area is drying at the close of the rainy season, it is known by the common but appropriate name of Farewell-to-Spring (Clarkia purpurea ssp. quadrivulnera). The predominant color is lavender, often verging on a deep pink, with a spot of deeper tone near the base of each of the four petals. It prefers brushy or wooded areas and competes with the tall grass by growing on slender stems 1 to 3 feet long. The species illustrated is very similar in color and form, but may be distinguished from Clarkia purpurea ssp. quadrivulnera by the pendulous buds. It is identified as Clarkia dudleyana.

One of the most common and typical of California wildflowers is the lupine, a member of the pea family. It is found from seacoast to mountain peak and occurs in many widely varying species. Most lupine blossoms are in shades of blue, red-violet or purple, although some lupines are yellow, others white and one (Harlequin Lupine —Lupinus stiversii) has the unusual color combination of yellow and pink in a single blossom. As one drives through the foothills to Yosemite in April, one of the most impressive flower spectacles between 2,000 and 4,000 feet is the Bush Lupine (Lupinus albifrons), forming great rounded masses of magenta-purple, the long blooming spikes often tipped with silvery gray where the individual blossoms are still in bud. The shrubs may reach heights of 4 to 5 feet. Their leaves are in the spreading palmate form so typical of lupine, silvery-hairy in texture, light green in color. They seem to enjoy the roadsides and will frequent rocky cuts; they are indeed worthy forerunners of the scenic grandeur and floral beauty which lie ahead.

A drive up the Merced River Canyon along State Highway #140 from mid-March to mid-April will be rewarded by one of the most colorful flowering displays of the year. This is the time when the Western Redbud (Cercis occidentalis) comes into bloom, and its small, boat-shaped, magenta-colored blossoms produce great mounds of brilliance on the tree-sized shrubs growing along the river. As the leaves do not appear until the flowers have begun to fade, there is nothing to compete with the tremendous surge of color. Later, the rounded, bright green leaves appear, and the shrubs are attractive in that aspect as well. Throughout the summer, the long, rusty-red seed pods hang on the branches, themselves giving almost a blossoming effect.

Another shrub or small tree frequently seen along the Merced Canyon puts out its long, slender leaves in startling green of a deeply saturated quality as the redbud blossoms reach their peak of magenta color. This is the California Buckeye (Aesculus californica), sometimes referred to as "horse chestnut" because of the spectacular brown fruits or nuts which form in late summer. The blending of the green tone of these leaves with the magenta of the redbud is a truly satisfying experience in color imagery. Later in May or early June, long spikes of creamy white blossoms appear in quantity across the rounded profiles of these small shrub-like trees. The spikes are 4 to 6 inches in length, numerous on each tree, and are spectacularly apparent as one drives along the Merced Canyon on Highway #140. They may also be seen from Highway #41 out of Fresno, although not as frequently. The buckeye's range is between 1,000 and 3,000 feet. Summer visitors will notice these trees, too, for they follow the unusual pattern of shedding their leaves at the onset of the dry season—the only deciduous tree of this region which responds in this manner to the hot, dry foothill summers. With the leaves gone, the large shiny brown seed pods or fruits hang prominently from the branches like decorative ornaments on a Christmas tree.

California Poppies *(Eschscholzia californica)* frequently make striking springtime displays of orange-gold on the grassy hillsides on any of the approach roads to Yosemite, usually appearing in April. In good wildflower years they are especially dramatic on the steep canyon slopes along the Merced River on Highway #140. It is the California state flower, occurring in grassy, open areas from sea level to nearly 5,000 feet. These brilliant flower cups, up to 2 inches across, consist of 4 petals lifted to the sunlight on stems 9 to 24 inches high, rising from a mass of silvery green leaves divided into numerous fine segments. When poppies grow intermixed with short-stemmed ground lupines, the contrast of orange and blue presents one of the most scintillating effects in the world of wildflowers. Enjoy your poppies in the mid-day sun, for they close their flower cups in late afternoon and do not reopen until the morning sunshine floods them again with warmth. On overcast days, usually they don't open at all.

One of California's most typical shrubs, manzanita, is encountered frequently on any of the three approach roads to Yosemite from the west. There are more than forty species of this shrub in the state, and the one most commonly seen on the foothills of the Sierra is the White-Leaf Manzanita *(Arctostaphylos viscida)*. It is a handsome type, by any standard, and visitors to Yosemite invariably are impressed by its satin-smooth, maroon-colored trunks and branches, thickly covered by small, roundish, gray leaves. These leaves provide the perfect color complement for the clusters of small pink blossoms which hang on the shrub in abundance, like tiny urns with delicate recurved lobes at the throat, from February to April. In midsummer, the blossoms mature as clusters of small, round, russet fruits, bearing a strong resemblance to little apples. The plant derives its name from these fruits, for "manzanita" in Spanish means, literally, "little apple." At any time of the year the shrub is an attractive landscape addition, its contorted maroon branches often reaching heights of 8 to 12 feet to form small trees. Other species of manzanita are to be found to the 10,000 foot elevation in Yosemite National Park.

A very colorful addition to the roadsides through the foothills and up to 5,000 feet is the little orange-crimson flower called Indian Pink or Catchfly *(Silene californica)*. It prefers brushy or wooded places and is seen near Wawona, on Highway #41, and along Highway #120 west of the Park boundary. Occasionally one finds it in the Merced Canyon, too, along Highway #140. This little beauty appears on stems from 5 to 16 inches high, several arising from a single rootstock. The unusually bright-colored blossom forms a tube which flares out in a flat plane about an inch in diameter, with deeply scalloped, or "pinked," edges. Look for it in April and May.

Even the casual observer will notice a number of other species not listed above along one of the approach roads to Yosemite in April and early May. Mary Curry Tresidder, writing in her typically sensitive manner about the coming of springtime

11

to the Sierran foothills, calls attention to a further list of seasonal favorites which anyone with eyes to see will be sure to admire:

"At this season, the poppy-colored fiddleneck *(Amsinckia intermedia* var. *eastwoodae),* in the fields and along the roadsides approaching the Sierran foothills, is one of the fine displays between Merced or Fresno and Yosemite. The dusty-leaved foothill species of California lilac *(Ceanothus cuneatus)* has begun to blossom from the Mariposa region upward, and in a few days more it will be showing its rounded creamy bouquets throughout the fields.

"In the moist cuts where water drips from the rocks after a wet winter there are many small treasures such as dwarf shooting stars *(Dodecatheon hansenii);* sometimes the small-flowered brodiaea known as 'blue dicks' or 'grass nuts' *(Brodiaea pulchella)* fringe the rocks in grassy pockets, or a few scarlet paintbrush *(Castilleja applegatei)* may have ventured out already. An occasional stonecrop *(Dudleya cymosa)* is already spreading its succulent rosettes of pale green leaves on rocky places that are less fertile, but they have not yet turned to their yellow-ochre coloring nor put up their bright scarlet flowers.

"This is really the period of the year to explore the network of foothill roads, careless of time and speed, in order to observe the embroidery of color on roadsides and flowery fields before the grasses get too high. One finds larkspur *(Delphinium hansenii)* and golden stars *(Brodiaea lutea* var. *scabra)* in the light shade of blue oaks or sparse digger pines, Chinese pagodas *(Collinsia heterophylla),* white popcorn flowers *(Plagiobothrys nothofulvus),* cream cups *(Platystemon californicus)* and tidy tips *(Layia fremontii)* in the open and along the fences, calico flowers or five-spot *(Nemophila maculata),* a cousin of the baby-blue-eyes, in patches here and there, and half a dozen assorted brodiaeas and gilias. Blazing star *(Mentzelia lindleyi* ssp. *crocea)* shows its dazzling yellow on the hillsides near Oakhurst and on some of the side roads of the Mariposa area or along the lower Big Oak Flat Road. The 'slippery ellum,' or flannel-bush *(Fremontia californica),* is a fairly common golden-flowered shrub blooming in April near Oakhurst on Highway #41."

Springtime in the foothills of the Sierra—March, April and early May—is a happy season, replete with endless vistas of lawn-green hillslopes, scatter rugs of floral color, bird songs, running streams in gullies and small canyons and long days of sunshine gradually warming toward the intensity of summer. By the end of May, the spring rains have ceased, the high-angled sun shines hotly and the grasses mature to a golden sheen as the flowers fade. Summer has arrived in the foothills; spring has moved on, up the mountain slopes, painting with wildflowers the meadows and canyons of the higher, more spectacular regions.

Golden Brodiaea

Tidy Tips

Fairy Lantern

Baby-Blue-Eyes

Bush Lupine

Clarkia

13

Redbud

Buckeye

Whiteleaf Manzanita

Indian Pink

California Poppy

14

Stonecrop

Five-Spot

Chinese Pagodas

Blazing Star

Flannel Bush

FLOWERS
OF
YOSEMITE VALLEY

In late April, while springtime is yet evident in the foothills of the Sierra, its forerunners are to be seen in Yosemite Valley. Although most of the flowers come somewhat later, April sets the tone of the happy season with the greening of the meadows and the bursting of leaf buds on the shrubs and broad-leaved trees. As Mary Tresidder writes so picturesquely: "Two of the delightful components of the early spring landscape are the delicate chartreuse-to-light-green tassels of the big-leaf maple, and the somewhat more russet tassels and unfolding ochre and scarlet leaves of the Kellogg black oak. The whip-like crimson stems of the creek dogwood, or red-osier dogwood, found in moist places, are another highlight of the picture, as its leaves begin to uncurl."

May is the month of full-blown springtime in the Valley, the time of tumultuous water in the famous falls and in the Merced River, the month when all growing things —grasses, ferns, flowers, shrubs, trees—literally gleam with the radiance of new growth. The full moon of May, shining on the peak volume of Yosemite Falls which pours over the Valley's rim in clouds of misty spray, produces that rarest of spectral images, a lunar rainbow at the foot of the Lower Fall. This month sees the start of the Valley's flowering season which then continues, in a succession of different blooming species, until August, even while spring continues its upward course toward the summit peaks.

One of the very first springtime blossoms is that perennial favorite, the violet. Preferring the filtered shade of the forest, there are three species of yellow violets in Yosemite. Perhaps the most commonly seen one is called simply the Mountain Violet (Viola purpurea). The yellow blossoms have purplish markings on the backs of the upper two petals and purple stripes on the lower three petals. The stems are 2 to 6

Cow Parsnip, Azalea in Yosemite Valley meadow

inches high, above a rosette of deep green, wedge-shaped leaves. It begins to bloom in the latter half of April and is commonly found in well-drained flats or slopes where the humus of centuries of leaves has enriched the soil. Near Happy Isles and along the trail to Inspiration Point are two typical locations. The dainty little Purple Violet *(Viola adunca)* may be found in the grass at the edge of meadows (Bridalveil Meadow, for instance), while Yosemite's only White Violet *(Viola macloskeyi)* prefers the more moist, tall-grass meadow locations such as in Leidig Meadow.

The one flower most usually identified with the image of springtime in the memory of Yosemite's visitors is the Mountain Dogwood *(Cornus nuttallii)*. In years of early-arriving springs, the first of the large, white blossoms appear toward the end of April, but the month of May is the period which normally belongs to the dogwood, in all its glory, year in and year out. One can confidently expect to find these delicate blooms at their best in May, just as the peak of Yosemite's waterfalls can also be enjoyed in that favored month. Dogwood prefers damp places, so look for it near the Merced River's banks or along tributary streams. The area near Fern Spring, at Happy Isles and along Tenaya Creek below Mirror Lake are typical locations.

A strange flower is the dogwood. The flower actually consists of the small center button—a tight head of many tiny florets which turn lemon-yellow in bloom and produce a cluster of bright red seeds in September, a favorite food for robins and other birds. What appear to be large white petals are instead showy bracts surrounding the flower cluster. The effect, however, when the dogwood trees are in full bloom, is of gigantic snowflakes drifting through the contrasting dark green of the coniferous forest, a picture of rare beauty which will be ever associated with the memory of springtime in Yosemite. Dogwood is properly classified as a tree, yet its blossoms are always included in any listing of Yosemite's most popular blooms.

When the dogwood begins to fade, the Western Azalea (*Rhododendron occidentale*) comes into its prime. As the month of May belongs to the dogwood, so is June the season for azalea. This handsome deciduous shrub is widely spread throughout much of California, but rarely does it achieve a finer impression of vitality and beauty than in the meadows of Yosemite Valley. It thrives in full sunlight and moderately moist, acid soil—thus making it an ideal meadow plant, especially where oak leaves have created rich humus. One of the finest locations for azalea is the El Capitan Meadow where in one area there is an extensive thicket of bushes—3 to 8 feet high. In June, the rich fragrance of their blossoms pervades the meadow, and the brightness of the large flower clusters is the dominant tone in the landscape. The individual flowers are creamy white, with a spot of yellow on the upper portion of the funnel-form blossom, which is 1½ to 2 inches long. Unopened buds are strikingly outlined in pink, and often some of this color appears as a faint tinge on the blossom. In late October, the leaves turn to gold, orange or red, creating one of the most prominent tones in the landscape of autumn. Azalea may be found up to 7,000 feet, along the Glacier Point and Tioga Roads in July, but it is seen at its best in the lovely meadows of Yosemite Valley.

The most vividly colorful of the Valley flowers is, without doubt, the Snow Plant (*Sarcodes sanguinea*). When it begins to emerge through the forest floor in early May, it resembles a large red asparagus stem with many slender red leaves tightly wrapped around. As the plant grows, bell-shaped red flowers appear at the top of the stem in a terminal raceme, the plant thus reaching its final blooming phase in about 3 weeks. The snow plant is of surpassing interest to flower fanciers and photographers at all stages of its development, because of its deeply saturated red tone throughout. It lacks the chlorophyll which gives the familiar green color to most plants, and which is essential to the production of plant food. Hence, it derives its nourishment from decaying organic material under the forest floor and is classified as a saprophyte. Look for this spectacular flower from May to July, first on the floor of Yosemite Valley, later in the Mariposa Grove of Sequoias and along the Glacier Point Road. It prefers areas of deep forest duff, under pines or firs, so it is hidden away from casual viewing. Nevertheless, each spring includes at least a few snow plants (in favorable years, multiple groupings may be found), and the thrill of discovery is more than ample reward for the search. Admire them you may and assuredly will, but there is a heavy fine for picking or otherwise disturbing one of these rare beauties.

Another saprophyte which blooms slightly later than the snow plant is the strange Pinedrop (*Pterospora andromedea*). In June, you may find it growing (as the name suggests) under the Ponderosa pines. It is said to be parasitic on the fungi that are symbiotically associated with the tree roots. Pinedrops appear as tall wand-like stalks, rust colored, somewhat sticky with small, brown, scale-like leaves. It may grow to a height of 1 to 3 feet flowering from June to August. The flowers hang pendent along the upper portion of the stalk, like small bells, and vary in color from white to red. After flowering, the plant dies, but its warm-toned stalks stand like exclamation points in the forest far into the fall and winter. Its appearance in Yosemite Valley is intermittent and cannot be as precisely pinpointed as with some flowers, yet at least a few of these unusual plants are to be found every year.

April brings one of the early and exceedingly attractive harbingers of spring, the

Bleeding Heart *(Dicentra formosa),* found in moist, shaded areas and along small streams. Near Fern Spring, the river bank oozes with the water from a number of large and small springs, creating an ideal habitat under the filtered shade of tall pines, firs and cedars. The rose-purple flowers grow on stems a foot or more high, nodding gracefully above a cluster of large leaves which are much dissected. The blossoms have four petals which combine to form an elongated heart, with two small spurs at the base. Though seen nowhere in abundance, where conditions are right, it grows up to an elevation of 6,000 feet. Two other interesting members of this genus are found in Yosemite: Golden Ear-Drops *(Dicentra chrysantha),* a tall stalk with bright yellow flowers seen along the Big Oak Flat Road above the second tunnel, and Steer's Head *(Dicentra uniflora),* a tiny white replica of a bleached steer's skull which appears just after the snow has left the ground from 7,000 to 10,500 feet.

In deep shady woods, rich in humus, look for the handsome large leaves of the Wild Ginger *(Asarum hartwegii),* which are roughly heart-shaped and a rich, glossy green. Parting these leaves carefully you will find one of the most pleasing of springtime surprises—a little group of brownish-purple faces peering up at you elfishly. These blossoms are found at ground level (actually the plant is stemless) and are well hidden beneath the spreading canopy of leaves. They are little cups, the exterior quite hairy, and with elongated tips at the end of each of the three sepals. (This blossom has no true petals.) The aromatic quality of the leaves and roots is reminiscent of commercial ginger which, however, is a tropical plant. Wild ginger was used as a substitute for the imported type by early settlers. You will be agreeably surprised by its fragrance in addition to its interesting form; rub your fingers briskly across a leaf to enjoy its spicy aroma. A typical place to find wild ginger, in May and June, is along the trail from Mirror Lake to Snow Creek Falls, in Tenaya Canyon.

The warm days of late May and June—early summer—bring out carpets of Pussy Paws *(Calyptridium umbellatum)* across the open, gravelly, sun-drenched flats in portions of Yosemite Valley. They are often seen, for instance, along the incoming South Side Drive near the start of the Four-Mile Trail. In spite of its common occurrence this little blossom never ceases to merit admiration from Park visitors for its rosettes of pink to white flower heads rising from a circle of bright green leaves. The heads, usually 1 to 2 inches across, are made up of innumerable tiny flowers crowded together, giving a total effect of softness which has been likened to the upturned paw of a kitten. The flower stems varying from 2 to 10 inches long, rise from the basal leaves to hold the blooms somewhat erect during the warmth of daytime but generally return to a prone position with the cool of evening. Pussy paws are hardy little plants and can be found growing all the way to tree line, wherever soil and sun are suitable.

With the advent of summer's warm days, the maturing of the Valley meadows brings a climax of flowering. One of summer's favorites, which decorates the meadows in subtle tones of rose and silver-gray, is the Showy Milkweed *(Asclepias speciosa).* Its tall stalks, 2 to 4 feet high, hold large sprays of blossoms, individually small but forming umbels (clusters of flowers with all the divisional stems arising from one point) 4 to 6 inches across. The long leaves, covered with woolly hairs, produce an interesting effect in themselves and add a soft shade of green which complements the rose-purple of the flowers. In autumn, these leaves turn a bright yellow, while each flower stalk is conspicuous for the large woolly pods which finally

19

split and release their myriads of seeds—each seed equipped with a mass of silken fibres which enable it to drift across the landscape on the gentlest breeze. The handsome Monarch butterfly is especially attracted to this milkweed, its caterpillars feeding on the leaves and absorbing a bitter poison which makes them unattractive to birds. You will find this showy flower in masses in Yosemite's meadows in June and July, especially in the Ahwahnee Meadow.

At about the same time, another common but very conspicuous plant comes into bloom. Preferring moist areas of meadows, the Cow Parsnip *(Heracleum lanatum)* grows in a profusion of creamy white blossoms on tall, coarse stalks with deeply toothed large leaves up to 12 inches across. The blossom consists of a broad, flat umbel which in turn is made up of 15 to 30 smaller umbels of tiny blooms. The whole effect is of a large design in lace work. Although the entire plant is big and coarse, a grouping of these showy members of the carrot family in a grassy meadow, with the background of Yosemite's cliffs and waterfalls, is a memory to cherish. It is prominent in the Valley meadows in June (often especially lush in Cook's and Sentinel Meadows) and may be found in moist locations up to 8,000 feet later in the summer.

From late May until the early frosts of autumn, a frequently seen flower in wet areas of meadows and along stream banks is the little Sneezeweed *(Helenium bigelovii)*. Sunflower yellow, it grows on slender stems 1 to 2 feet high, its flower head a tight grouping of minute yellow-brown florets surrounded by 13 to 30 bright golden rays which droop slightly to form a fringe. The resemblance to our common sunflower *(Helianthus annuus)* is marked, yet the little sneezeweed has an erect and vivacious quality which instantly sets it apart. A large display is usually seen in Cook's Meadow in June, and it can also be found during the summer months along the Merced River below Happy Isles. Don't be alarmed by the common name of this charming flower; few persons if any have been known to develop allergic reactions in its presence. The name was derived from its early use by pioneers, who are said to have dried the flower, powdered it and used it to produce sneezing in an attempt to relieve the congestion of head colds.

Occasionally found in Yosemite Valley in July is a delicate little flower in the wintergreen family, called Pipsissewa, or Prince's Pine *(Chimaphila umbellata* var. *occidentalis)*. Its bright green, waxy, elongated and toothed leaves clothe a stalk 6 to 12 inches high, from which arises a flower stem bearing from 3 to 7 small pink blossoms about the size of a nickel. They too have a waxy quality which causes them to gleam in the forest shadows. Pipsissewa flourishes in dry areas in the shady forests and is most likely to be found among the talus slopes at the base of Yosemite's cliffs. A colony of this distinctive little plant gives the impression of a miniature forest, while its neat, well-groomed appearance imparts to it something of a regal character. No wonder that Mary Tresidder, who admired this flower so much, chose it as her floral pseudonym one summer (each of her friends similarly selecting a flower name), calling herself "Princess Pipsissewa."

Among the shrubs in bloom in Yosemite Valley during May and June, one in particular is certain to provoke questions by visitors whose interests run to matters botanical. Its bright maroon-red blossoms, sprinkled liberally among the large green leaves identify the Spice Bush or Sweet Shrub *(Calycanthus occidentalis)*. This shrub may be quite large, growing to heights of 6 to 8 feet, with a generally rounded profile. The conspicuous red flowers form no great masses, but are borne at frequent intervals along the branches; they are succeeded by equally noticeable beige-colored seed pods about an inch long, resembling thimbles. Spice bush is so called because of the pleasant aroma of the twig ends when bruised or crushed. The flowers, however, have a distinctly unpleasant odor and seem to be in direct contradiction to its common name. You will find this shrub growing intermittently along the Merced River, more commonly below the level of Yosemite Valley. A large individual occurs at the road intersection near Curry Village. It has also been used quite effectively in the natural landscaping at Yosemite Lodge and The Ahwahnee Hotel.

In June, when the meadow grasses begin to mature, look for the rich blue-violet of Harvest Brodiaea *(Brodiaea elegans)*. Its slender stems, up to 16 inches high, hold at their apex richly toned flowers with funnel-like tubes, the lavender petals recurved at their tips like lilies. It is a gracefully formed plant which does indeed give an elegant appearance, as the scientific name suggests. There are usually several of these handsome flowers on each stem, but the plant does not create large masses of color. The long, thin leaves normally die about the time the flowers appear, so that these beautiful blossoms seem to be a part of the grassy covering of the meadows. They are often seen in the meadow near the Devil's Elbow beach, intermingled with the rose-purple of godetia. This brodiaea was a favored food of the Indians, who dug the bulbs and cooked them in earthen ovens.

Another little meadow flower of midsummer, an attractive member of the gentian family, can be found in sunny, grassy flats on the Valley floor. This is the Canchalagua *(Centaurium venustum* ssp. *abramsii)*, a showy little blossom in spite of its rather short stems (4 to 12 inches high). Its rose-magenta flowers have five-pointed petals surrounding a white throat with red spots, the whole being less than an inch across. These small blossoms are best seen and most appreciated at close range, but they also create mass effects of great color intensity under favorable conditions. The western end of El Capitan Meadow and the grassy expanse of shoreline to the north of Mirror Lake are two good places to look for them.

Walk out into almost any of the meadows of Yosemite Valley in July, and you are likely to encounter the tall stalks of St. John's Wort *(Hypericum formosum* var. *scouleri)*. It has erect stems up to two feet high, surmounted by clusters of bright yellow flowers about an inch across, with many stamens which give to the blossom a bristly appearance. The rather short leaves are paired and are black-dotted along the margins. From midsummer on there are many yellow flowers which come into bloom and, at some distance, St. John's Wort seems rather undistinguished—neither more nor less interesting than the rest. However, at close range, its intricate structure and brightly lacquered color make it one of the more attractive of summer's offerings. You will be glad to have made its acquaintance.

In the same meadowy areas, and at about the same time, expect to find another yellow flower, a very familiar one to many people. The Black-Eyed Susan *(Rudbeckia hirta* var. *pulcherrima)* is typically a plant of the eastern United States and was probably brought west by early settlers who brewed it to make a medicinal tea. It has readily adapted itself to the western mountains and is quite commonly found in Yosemite's meadows, where it blooms profusely throughout the summer months and into early autumn. Long, golden rays surround a central disc of deep brown, creating a flower 2 to 3 inches across on erect stems 2 to 4 feet high. Its leaves, 2 to 4 inches long, are covered with a sheen of fine silvery hairs. For many visitors to

Yosemite, this meeting with an old friend from back home adds pleasure to their Park experience.

Still another prominent yellow flower of summer is the Evening Primrose *(Oenothera hookeri)*. As the name implies, it blooms in the evening and fades with the warming sun of the following morning. For a short time in the morning light, its delicate yellow blossoms—2 to 3 inches wide—may be enjoyed to the fullest, a favorite subject for photographers. The stout stems with long, lance-shaped leaves rise 3 to 6 feet high, bearing what seem to be limitless quantities of buds. Only a few open each evening, however, so the lovely primrose contrives to remain a vivid part of summer's floral displays well into September. To watch the opening of a primrose blossom on a summer evening is a fascinating experience. Within a few minutes the sepals fold back, revealing the gold color beneath. Gradually, the four petals uncurl to form the completed flower—the entire transition from bud to blossom having occurred before your astonished gaze. The flowers emit a perfume which can attract a sphinx moth from several hundred feet away; these graceful creatures are of course an important element in the pollination of the evening primrose. Deer relish the primrose buds for browse and have effectively eliminated the plant from many meadow areas in Yosemite Valley where they once were abundant. However, this handsome flower has been used extensively in the landscaping around The Ahwahnee Hotel and Yosemite Lodge and may be seen there in great numbers.

One of Yosemite's most commonly seen white flowers throughout much of the Park, and especially in the Valley, is the Yarrow *(Achillea lanulosa)*. In the sunflower family, it has 4 to 6 white petal-like rays surrounding a buff-colored disc of tiny florets. The whole flower is less than a half-inch across, but is arranged with numerous others to form flat-topped terminal clusters of bloom, 2 to 4 inches wide, which at a slight distance appear to be a compound flower-head. The stems are erect, 2 to 3 feet high, and are thickly clothed with leaves. These leaves are one of the more interesting characteristics of the yarrow. They are intricately divided into many finely cut, delicate leaflets which give to the plant another common name: Milfoil or, literally, a "thousand leaves." Looking somewhat like fern fronds and quite aromatic, these distinctive leaves are readily noticed from early spring until late fall and serve to identify the white yarrow most of the year. Look for it in any of Yosemite Valley's meadows throughout the summer in rather dry, open areas.

When summer wanes, two flowers become prominent in the meadows and along roadsides in Yosemite Valley. One is lavender in color, one is old gold; as they are sometimes seen in the same area, the contrast is dramatic and very pleasing indeed. The lavender one is Sierra Lessingia *(Lessingia leptoclada)*. Mary Tresidder had a beautifully descriptive common name for it: "summer lavender." Its tiny flowers produce mass effects on dry flats, or sometimes as hedgerows along roadsides, that give the illusion of a thin veil or ground mist of purest color floating across the landscape. At closer range, however, lessingia appears very much like a tiny aster, to which it is distantly related, as both are in the composite or sunflower family. The small flowers are borne at the tips of the branchlets; as the mature plants are a mass of branching and re-branching stems, one gets the impression of a mound of delicate color. Lessingia first appears in late June as a single short stem a few inches high, with a solitary bloom at its tip. Thereafter, the growing and branching occurs steadily, so that by the end of August it will be about 2 feet in height. A very typical location to see it at its best is the southern side of the Ahwahnee Meadow, where it reaches its peak about Labor Day.

The golden-colored blossom is, of course, that well-known harbinger of autumn, Meadow Goldenrod *(Solidago canadensis* ssp. *elongata)*. Actually, the first blossoms appear in midsummer, but it continues to bloom until the end of September, making lines of gold across the Valley meadows which by that time are also maturing their grasses in warm tones of ochre and orange. Goldenrod is a mass of tiny yellow flower heads in small compact clusters which form spikes of blossoms 3 to 7 inches long. The stems vary from 12 to 40 inches in height, are quite hairy and have many long, sharply notched leaves. As beautiful as this plant is in full bloom, many people are wary of it because it is popularly reputed to be a cause of hay fever. This is rarely true, however, for the sticky grains of pollen are carried by insects and not distributed by the wind. Most of Yosemite's meadows produce good showings of goldenrod, but there are often exceptional displays in Bridalveil and Stoneman Meadows.

In addition to the more noticeable of Yosemite Valley's wildflowers which are pictured herein and described above, sharp eyes will find many others during the flowering months of May, June and July. Certain to be encountered by anyone who is sincerely interested are such diverse beauties as: the unusual pink and yellow Harlequin Lupine *(Lupinus stiversii)*; the Mariposa Lily, with its cup-shaped flower-head of gleaming white *(Calochortus leichtlinii)*; the Purple Milkweed *(Asclepias cordifolia)*; the white, waxy blossoms of Syringa or Mock Orange, a fragrant shrub *(Philadelphus lewisii* ssp. *californicus)*; Blue Penstemon *(Penstemon laetus)*, sometimes remarkably lavender, in dry areas; the pale purple blossoms of the Giant Hyssop *(Agastache urticifolia)*, an aromatic member of the mint family; Yerba Santa *(Eriodictyon californicum)*, a woody plant with masses of small tubular lavender flowers; Chinese Houses *(Collinsia tinctoria)*, erect stalks of white flowers rising in whorls; Elderberry *(Sambucus caerulea)*, a large shrub with flat masses of yellow flowers, maturing to blue berries; Shieldleaf *(Streptanthus tortuosus)* with tiny purple flowers and conspicuous round yellow leaves.

The wildflower enthusiast will find some blossoming on the floor of Yosemite Valley until the end of August, but the months of May and June are the period of finest displays. By early July, the higher elevations of the Park are becoming free of snow and spring arrives there, providing the proper conditions for a whole new sequence of flowers. Thus the happy season progresses from week to week.

Let's follow along!

Mountain Violet

Mountain Dogwood

Western Azalea

Snow Plant

Pinedrops

Wild Ginger

Bleeding Heart

Pussy Paws

Showy Milkweed

Cow Parsnip

Sneezeweed

Harvest Brodiaea

Pipsissewa

St. John's Wort

Spice Bush

Black-Eyed Susan

Canchalagua

Evening Primrose

White Yarrow

Sierra Lessingia

Goldenrod

Harlequin Lupine

Syringa or Mock Orange

Giant Hyssop

27

ALONG
VALLEY RIM
TRAILS

The rims of this famous chasm, Yosemite Valley, rise more than 3,000 feet above the level parklands of its floor—creating a landscape of forests, meadows and granite domes amid a very different environment from the Valley itself. Here, on plateaus between 7,000 and 8,000 feet in elevation, we enter the region sometimes referred to as the Canadian Zone, since its flora and fauna resemble those found at the latitude of southern Canada. Another system of life zone classification, keyed more closely to the dominant plants of each area, refers to this rim country as the Lodgepole Pine-Red Fir Belt. These two trees are indeed prominent in the forests at this elevation but in addition we find—in some quantity—Jeffrey pines, western white pines (sometimes called silver pines), Sierra juniper and aspen. The stately Big Tree, or *Sequoiadendron giganteum,* occurs just below this zone, reaching elevations in Yosemite National Park up to 6,500 feet, while another noble tree, the sugar pine, also flourishes at elevations just under the rim country.

This is a region of magnificent forests, embellished with silken green meadows, as well as open, gravelly slopes rolling up to the massive domes which are so typical of the middle elevations of the Park. Here and there small streams glide downward toward the Valley rims—streams with such memorable names as Yosemite Creek, Bridalveil Creek, Ribbon Creek, Sentinel Creek, Illilouette Creek—the very streams which fling themselves over these rims to drift down in misty columns of spray to the Valley floor as the famous waterfalls of Yosemite. In this splendid rim country is a unique combination of differing wildflower habitats: the moist meadows and stream-banks—the dry, sun-drenched rocky slopes or "gravel gardens"—the deeply shaded humus of the forest floor under the red firs and lodgepoles. Thus perfect conditions are provided for a wide variety of flowering plants.

Yampah in Peregoy Meadow

There is a network of trails along each rim which will enable the hiker to penetrate as much of the region as he desires to see. For those not so inclined, or physically unable to walk this much at higher elevations, two fine roads permit driving through some representative portions of the best of the rim country. The Glacier Point Road follows along the plateau to the south of Yosemite Valley, reaching a maximum elevation of 8,000 feet and finally coming out to the rim itself at Glacier Point, 7,300 feet in elevation and directly above Curry Village, far below. To the north of the Valley, the Tioga Road climbs up to the rim and beyond, threading its way through a magnificent granite wilderness which is the approach to the eastern gateway of Yosemite National Park at the 9,941-foot Tioga Pass.

Let's do a bit of flower hunting along these roads. After that, we'll hike down the Pohono Trail which extends 13 miles along the south rim of Yosemite Valley, from Glacier Point to the Wawona Road at the tunnel. A walk on this trail, in mid-July, can provide one of the finest of wildflower adventures.

As one drives from Yosemite Valley up either of the two roads to the rim country in June or early July, one of the shrubs most certain to attract attention is the Deer Brush *(Ceanothus integerrimus)*. Its small ovate leaves and tender stems are a favorite browse for deer. The fluffy panicles of white flowers, occasionally tinged with blue, resemble the form of the domestic lilac, hence another common name, California Lilac. This shrub may grow to heights of 10 to 12 feet and is encountered in quantity on mountain slopes between 5,000 and 7,000 feet elevation.

Several other species of ceanothus also are found in this area. A lower growing form produces powder-blue flowers and is more commonly seen along the Big Oak Flat Road below Crane Flat. Near Chinquapin, on the Wawona Road, a prostrate shrub called Fresno Ceanothus, or Fresno Mat *(Ceanothus fresnensis)*, spreads across the open rocky slopes on the roadsides, with mats of tiny blue flowers scarcely raised above the foliage. Another type, also somewhat prostrate, but making wide shrubby mounds under the red fir forest, is the Snow Bush *(Ceanothus cordulatus)*. Its blossoms make great heaps of white under the firs, resembling late-lying drifts of last winter's snow.

Above the Wawona Tunnel, along the Glacier Point Road in June and July, a tall, slender plume of white waves in the breeze. This is Alum-Root *(Heuchera micrantha var. erubescens)*, in the saxifrage family and somewhat reminiscent of that familiar garden flower, coral-bells. Rising out of a rosette of roundish, somewhat lobed leaves, the flower stalks, 1 to 2 feet high, produce panicles of minute white flowers, so delicate they seem to float unattached. This unusually graceful flower prefers dry rocky places, so it is often seen in road cuts and along trail sides. Even after the flowers have turned to seeds, the tall, silhouetted stalks and interestingly shaped leaves attract attention. In late summer, many of the leaves turn a bright red.

Another flower which often will be noticed as one drives either road in early- to mid-summer is the Blue Penstemon *(Penstemon laetus)*. Its long, tubular blossoms range from blue to purple, and the upper ends of the petals are recurved to form an ideal landing place for bees, an important element in the pollination of these flowers, as they busily go in and out during their unending search for honey. The plants send up many flowering stalks, 1 to 2 feet high, and in full bloom the effect is of a mound of color. They prefer dry, rocky areas, and the contrast between the deeply saturated blue-violet tones of these blossoms and their background of light gray granite is exceptionally pleasing. Roadsides are frequent habitats for this penstemon; along the Tioga Road near the crossing of Yosemite Creek is a place it may be seen to advantage every year.

One of Yosemite's most prized wildflowers occurs at moderate elevations along either road during July, the Washington Lily *(Lilium washingtonianum)*. Although never appearing in large numbers, this majestic white beauty can be found, to at least a limited extent, each summer. Look for it on steep, well-drained slopes, preferably where low shrubbery gives it the necessary cover to permit growth and flowering, safe from browsing deer. Long stalks—up to 6 feet tall—carry several of these exquisite, trumpet-shaped flowers, reminiscent of Easter lilies. The blossoms are 3 to 5 inches long. Delicately fragrant, they have the white purity of new snow, with a few reddish dots on the petals. The long, slender leaves are arranged in symmetrical whorls at intervals along the stalk, producing in themselves a pleasing geometric pattern. Altogether a thrilling sight is the Washington lily. Look for it along the Wawona Road for several miles on either side of Chinquapin, and also on the Tioga Road for a few miles on each side of Crane Flat.

Near Crane Flat, in July and August, expect to find that unusual member of the sunflower family, the California Coneflower *(Rudbeckia californica)*. Its tall stems, 2 to 6 feet high, raise the showy yellow flowers to a position where they are easily seen from the road. The sunflower-like blossoms are deep yellow, 4 to 6 inches across, the central discs of dark brown forming a cone 1 to 2 inches in height. No other sunflower in Yosemite has this distinctive feature in the blossom. For several weeks in midsummer during favorable years, the meadows near Crane Flat glow with its vibrant yellow. The coneflower may also be seen along the Wawona Road, though

30

less spectacularly, and there is a good showing of it near Chinquapin, the Glacier Point road junction.

Frequently seen along either route is a bright red, low-growing flower preferring rocky locations, where it has established itself in crevices—often high above the road. This is the familiar Mountain-Pride (Penstemon newberryi), a long-time favorite of those who know and love the high places of the Sierra Nevada. Its flowers are tubular, 1 to 1¹/₂ inches long, and occur in clusters on rather short, leafy stems which form masses of low foliage. During the period from late June to early August, mountain-pride is a familiar sight along roads and trails from 5,000 to 11,000 feet. Once you have identified it, this cheery little plant will be there to greet you again and again on many another mountain excursion.

One of the most pleasant aspects of the rim country is the number of fine mountain meadows to be enjoyed. Both roads and trails offer the traveler a splendid selection, and the month of July brings them to their peak of flowering beauty. The large meadow at Crane Flat and Summit Meadow on the Glacier Point Road are excellent examples. Each one has rather similar floral displays, the Crane Flat Meadow (which is somewhat lower in elevation) reaching its best stage in early July, with Summit Meadow doing so about two weeks later.

A dominant color in each area is the bright pink of the Shooting Star (Dodecatheon jeffreyi), which often is seen as a band of color across whole areas of the meadows' expanse. Viewed closely, too, it is of great interest for its shape as well as its exquisite coloring, the inch-long petals turning backwards from the cluster of stamens as though blown by a streamlining blast of wind. These petals are deeply pink to lavender, or sometimes almost white, with yellow at the base and outlined by a maroon band. The flower stalks are erect, 6 to 20 inches high, and arise from a rosette of roundish basal leaves. Shooting stars, with small variations, are found from the foothill zone to 10,000 feet. This species, however, is the largest and most splendid of the Yosemite varieties.

When the shooting stars are in their prime, another unusual flower will be found sharing the boggy meadow areas. This one is the Camas Lily (Camassia leichtlinii ssp. suksdorfii), a deep blue to violet blossom of true elegance. A single erect stem, 1 to 3 feet high, rises from a whorl of long basal leaves, bearing at its tip 4 to 12 blossoms. Each consists of 6 petals, long and pointed, star-like, surrounding 6 stamens with bright golden anthers at their tips. The contrast between this brilliant gold and the royal blue of the petals is striking, while the clean lines of the flower's structure make it especially graceful. Camas buds open late in the day, and the blossoms wither by the next day's light, so one should plan to seek them in the afternoon. A meadowy expanse of these richly colored blue-purple lilies, accented with pink shooting stars, is an experience not to be forgotten.

Another plant to look for in these bog-garden meadows is the Sierra Rein Orchid (Habenaria dilatata var. leucostachys), one of almost a dozen members of the orchid family in Yosemite National Park. It grows as a tall, thick stalk with clasping leaves, terminating in a spike of tiny, white flowers, each one about ¹/₂ inch long. These pillars of bloom stand 1 to 3 feet high in very wet areas, like ghostly accent marks to the meadows' flowering statements. Although the individual blossoms are very small, their structure leaves no doubt they are true orchids. They are found in moist areas from Yosemite Valley to 10,000 feet elevation, from late May to early August; Summit

Meadow, along the Glacier Point Road, is a typical habitat for them in July.

While wading into the boggy turf, look for another dweller in the wet grasslands, the Lungwort, sometimes called Mountain Bluebell *(Mertensia ciliata* var. *stomatechoides)*. On erect stems, 1 to 5 feet high, clusters of light blue flowers occur, often fading to pink. Their tendency to droop gracefully from the stem has given to them yet another common name, Languid Lady. Each blossom is a small bell-like tube about 1/2 inch long, a thing of beauty when seen in close-up, yet when the plant is in full bloom, it often makes masses of color. They prefer growing at the edge of moist meadows, rather than directly in the bog. One area in which they can be found is the upper or eastern end of the meadow at the Badger Pass ski bowl. The grassy expanse sloping down to Lukens Lake, one mile north of the Tioga Road, is also a prime location for the lungwort in early July.

Moist meadows are also the preferred habitat for another familiar Sierran plant, the Corn Lily or False Hellebore *(Veratrum californicum)*. Its tall stalks (up to 6 feet high) are commonly seen in Yosemite's meadows from 6,000 to 10,000 feet elevation in July and early August. A striking plant in all phases of its development, it has some resemblance to field corn, which tends to justify its common name, however superficially. As it first emerges from the meadow turf in June, its leaves are tightly wrapped around the stem, reminding one of an ear of corn which has been cut from the stalk and set down in the grass. The large, boat-shaped leaves open rapidly, finally becoming 10 to 16 inches long and 4 to 8 inches wide, with prominent ribs or veins. As the stalk attains its full height of 3 to 6 feet, it begins to "tassel out," again reminiscent of field corn. The "tassels" consist of many white flowers about 3/4 inch across, with Y-shaped glands at the base of each petal. They are precisely formed and beautiful to see in close-up, but make a memorable display in mass as the entire flower cluster comes into bloom. A meadow full of tall corn lilies resembles a statuary garden, each one an individual work of art in traditional creamy white. Crane Flat Meadow is usually well supplied with this flower, while along the Glacier Point Road you will find the Badger Pass Meadow a likely place.

That same meadow at Badger Pass is a good place to seek out one of the showiest of the mimulus—the Pink Monkeyflower *(Mimulus lewisii)*. Once seen, the blossom will not soon be forgotten, as its color harmonies feature a delicate pink to red tone with two brightly yellow, hairy ridges down the throat. It is a large flower, 1 to 2 inches long and 1/2 to 3/4 inches wide, usually borne in quantity on long stalks. The plant grows from 12 to 30 inches tall, producing numerous blossoms at the peak of its production. It is found in moist locations on the edge of meadows or along stream banks. When traveling the Tioga Road, look for it in July and early August along the roadside just before reaching Smoky Jack Campground.

Another mimulus will reward those who watch closely for interesting floral effects along the Wawona Road. This is the Scarlet Monkeyflower *(Mimulus cardinalis)*, one of the most brilliantly colored of Yosemite's hundreds of flowering plants. It is bright scarlet in tone, the petals conspicuously two-lipped, with the stamens protruding. The blossoms are about 2 inches in length, and when the plant is in full bloom (July and August) it bears many of these handsome flowers, which contrast vividly with its bright green leaves. The stems are many-branched and from 1 to 3 feet tall. A fine display may be seen about two miles north of the Chinquapin junction, at a place where small springs drip down the steep slope to make a bog garden at the roadside. Scarlet monkeyflower also grows profusely along Tenaya Creek in Yosemite Valley, a short distance above the Tenaya Bridge and, in fact, may be found rather widely distributed between 4,000 and 7,000 feet elevation.

Another resident in the wettest meadow locations is the Marsh Marigold (Caltha howellii). Its brightly lacquered round leaves with scalloped edges are one of the earliest signs of spring's approach, as winter's snow is reduced to isolated, shade-protected drifts and sky-blue pools of melt-water replace it. In early June, the first of the creamy white blossoms appear, bearing 6 to 10 sepals (this little flower has no true petals) and a central mass of bright yellow stamens. For several weeks they brighten the moist areas along the Glacier Point Road; Pothole Meadow just ahead of the Sentinel Dome trailhead is a reliable place to see them. Marsh marigolds appear at the tips of 4- to 12-inch naked stalks, rising from a rosette of basal leaves. After the flowers have turned to the cycle of seed-setting, these leaves grow to larger size and become an interesting part of the ground cover of damp meadows.

The drier meadows, too, have their own roster of plants which are to be found only in such locations and which are among the most frequently seen of Yosemite's flora. The bright blue-purple of Larkspur (Delphinium nuttallianum) is a prominent aspect of such meadows from June to August. Sometimes it gives deep violet tones to the landscape where myriads of blossoms occur together; in other locations only occasional purple spikes thrust skyward through the waving meadow grasses, on stems 8 to 24 inches tall. The blossoms are about an inch long, with 4 petals in unequal pairs. One of the 5 sepals is prolonged into an extended spur, the most distinctive feature of this plant, resembling the large spur on a lark's back toe. Peregoy Meadow, adjacent to the Bridalveil Creek Campground, is a likely place to find larkspur, although it may be glimpsed in many other locations along both the Glacier Point and Tioga Roads where open sunshine and moderately dry soil give it the conditions it requires.

Peregoy Meadow is also an excellent place in which to find that delicate little member of the carrot, or parsley family, Squaw Root or Yampah (Perideridia bolanderi). On stems 8 to 30 inches high, slender and almost leafless, the terminal flowers appear to float as small pieces of lace work. The individual blooms are minute, only 1/4 inch wide, but they form umbels of purest white up to 3 inches across. The almost-flat form of the blossom intensifies the lacy appearance which has suggested yet another common name, Queen Anne's Lace. Along the Tioga Road, look for it as a broad expanse of white in Crane Flat Meadow and 3 miles above at Gin Flat Meadow as well.

In moist meadows and along stream banks is another frequently seen resident of damp places. The bright yellow of the Arrowhead Groundsel (Senecio triangularis) on tall stalks—2 to 6 feet high—is a familiar sight from July to September. The flower heads are small, 1/2 inch across, but they are numerous, forming clusters of bloom at the tops of the stalks like golden torches across the landscape. The leaves are a distinctive feature of this plant, making it easy to distinguish from the dozen species of groundsel found in Yosemite National Park. They are from 2 to 8 inches long, with toothed edges and in a distinctly triangular form, which has given the species classification to this senecio. It often grows near areas of large perennial lupine of this altitude, the contrasting blue-lavender of lupine with bright gold of groundsel providing a classical study in complementary colors. Badger Pass Meadow has fine stands of this flower, but it may be found in quantity along either the Tioga or Glacier Point Road from 4,000 to 10,000 feet elevation.

One more dweller in the moist meadows is sure to be noticed, its rich tones of magenta or rose-purple making a pleasing accent in the scenery of summer. This is the Fireweed (Epilobium angustifolium), a plant of damp areas where forest fires, road work or clearings have removed other vegetation and given its wind-dispersed seeds a foothold. What a kindly provision has been made for the restoration of a devastated area, when flowers of such exquisite form and color can spring up so readily! This fireweed sends up tall stalks, 2 to 6 feet high, with many narrow leaves 3 to 5 inches long. The stalks end in racemes of bloom, clusters of 4-petalled flowers, deeply rose-purple, producing a climax of rich color. It reaches its peak in late July and in August. Look for it along the roadside near the junction to the Badger Pass Meadow. At Summit Meadow farther along the Glacier Point Road, fireweed is a prominent feature too. We will find a relative of this plant in the highest portion of the Park, at and above tree line in the rocky fell-fields.

Dry areas have their own species which brighten the roadsides and adjacent rocky slopes or may be found in the shade of deeply forested glens. One of the most prominent is the Sulphur Flower or Wild Buckwheat (Eriogonum umbellatum). Its varied shades of yellow and orange-red frequently are seen along either road between 6,000 and 9,000 feet, on open sunny flats, in granite sand. The plant is a mass of silvery gray stems, 4 to 12 inches high, rising out of a rosette of small leaves, smooth and green above but white-wooly below. At the tip of each stem is an umbrella-like flower head of many tiny florets, the whole about an inch across. The total effect is of a brilliantly colored small shrub, sometimes butter yellow and at others a rich orange, adding vibrant hues to the quiet grays of the granite landscape. A typical place to see it is at the Sentinel Dome trailhead on the Glacier Point Road. In Tuolumne Meadows, the sulphur flower is a common sight as well—frequently seen in the vicinity of the Soda Springs and along the start of the trail to Glen Aulin. Expect to find it in July and August.

At the Sentinel Dome trailhead, inconspicuous in the lodgepole pine forest to the east, one may often find excellent individual specimens of Davidson's Fritillary (Fritillaria pinetorum), an unusual and handsome member of the lily family, well worth a little time spent in searching for it. The richly colored flowers, warm bronze in tone with a greenish-yellow mottling, stand erect at the tips of slender stems, which are 5 to 14 inches tall. With 6 petals, each flower is about an inch wide, forming a bowl-shaped blossom of striking appearance. The leaves are as slender as the stems, often occurring in whorls. It blooms in June and July.

At Washburn Point, near the end of the Glacier Point Road, is an area memorable for a beautiful flower often called Sierra Forget-Me-Not (Hackelia velutina). Another common name, less romantic but derived from the burr-like nutlet which succeeds the flower, is Stickseed. On the well-drained, gravelly slope a short distance above and to the south of Washburn Point—from here is a fine view of the Clark Range and Illilouette Basin—bloom myriads of this attractive plant. Its color in this location is delicate pink, but in other areas the same flower may be the deep blue of a summer sky, or perhaps a hybrid tone between the two. At the top of stalks, 1 to 3 feet high, appears a cluster of blossoms, each one about 1/2 inch wide, blooming from late June to early August. The blue-colored version of this flower may be seen growing along the roadsides to the west of this point. An especially lush area for the deep blue forget-me-not is Crane Flat, where the Tioga Road turns east.

Travelers along the Wawona Road in late summer will notice occasional flashes of red by the roadside for some distance above the tunnel. This is the California Fuchsia (*Zauschneria californica* ssp. *latifolia*), a wildflower strongly reminiscent of the domesticated fuchsia so popular with gardeners. Tubular brick-red flowers, 1½ inches long, with a widely flaring throat and projecting stamens, bloom profusely from early August through September. The plants are a mass of branching, hairy stems, 12 to 36 inches high, with many gray-green pointed leaves. They prefer dry, gravelly locations and can often be found along roadsides or on open rocky slopes. This blossom is a favorite of hummingbirds, attracted by its red color.

From mid-June to mid-August, a drive along the Glacier Point Road will disclose many other flowering species besides those listed above—the number seemingly limited only by the time and interest the visitor has to devote to the subject. Certainly, one will notice: the tall shrubs of Bitter Cherry (*Prunus emarginata*) by the roadside, with many clusters of small, white, plum-like flowers; the much larger white flowers, 2 inches across, of Thimbleberry (*Rubus parviflorus*); tall spikes of orange-hued Wall-flower (*Erysimum capitatum*); wild Iris in variegated tones of buff and lavender (*Iris hartwegii*); Paintbrush (*Castilleja miniata*) flashing tall shafts of red-orange at the edge of damp meadows; the similar tone but strikingly different form of Colum-bine (*Aquilegia formosa*), distinctive red and yellow blossoms with long spurs; snow-white globes of Knotweed (*Polygonum bistortoides*) like stars among the meadow grasses; Western Pennyroyal (*Monardella lanceolata*), masses of gray-lavender blos-soms in dry areas; the low, shrub-like Dogbane (*Apocynum pumilum*) with myriads of small, pink, tubed flowers; Sierra Currant (*Ribes nevadense*), a shrub of stream banks with handsome clusters of small rose-red flowers; the bright yellow, convex leaves and tiny purple blossoms of Shieldleaf (*Streptanthus tortuosus*); Pearly Everlasting (*Anaphalis margaritacea*) raising its small, silvery gray flowers in hedgerows along the road; rounded bushes of Red Elderberry (*Sambucus microbotrys*), with creamy flowers in midsummer and bright red berries in September; mounds of Spreading Phlox (*Phlox diffusa*), star-like flowers ranging in color from white through pink to lilac on dry slopes or rocky flats; Mule-Ears (*Wyethia mollis*), with bright sunflower-like blooms on 2-foot stalks and long-stemmed woolly leaves.

The same magnificent company of wildflowers will greet the traveler as he drives up the Tioga Road, too. However, this one reaches elevations as much as 2,000 feet higher than the Glacier Point Road, so that plants of the subalpine belt, or Hudsonian Zone, are encountered as well. We will become acquainted with a number of them as we hike around the High Sierra Loop Trail from Tuolumne Meadows, covered in the next chapter.

Those who travel through this favored land should have not only eyes to see but also ears that hear the music of the forest and the meadows. Mary Tresidder had both to an unusual degree, plus the ability to set down her impressions with great clarity; she once wrote, "All through these woodlands and at the borders of the meadows, such as in the Crane Flat area, bird songs fill the air in early morning and late after-noon. Most likely to be heard, if not seen, will be fox sparrows, chickadees, purple finches, juncos, warblers and the scarlet and yellow tanager that flashes like a flame from one tree to another. An occasional rarity such as the hermit thrush, whose song

35

is in minor notes, may also be heard. Even the great gray owl has a favorite haunt or two in the area."

Before we turn from the rim country of Yosemite to the higher regions of the Park, let's leave our cars and follow a trail where the shyer wildflowers live, far away from asphalt and motor noises. We will walk the Pohono Trail; at the proper time, in mid-July, there is no finer display of wildflowers of the Lodgepole Pine-Red Fir belt to be seen anywhere. The trail is a long one, 13 miles on or near the south rim of Yosemite Valley, from Glacier Point to a junction with the Wawona Road at the east end of the Wawona Tunnel. It is possible to cut 3 miles off its total, by starting at the Sentinel Dome trailhead on the Glacier Point Road. But for our purposes let's start at Glacier Point itself and walk the entire distance. This can be done in one day by anyone who is in moderately good physical condition as the trail follows the gentle up-and-down contours of the rim with no difficult hills except for the last 2¹/₂ miles. Fortunately, for westbound hikers, this portion is downhill all the way to the tunnel.

Leaving Glacier Point, the trail climbs at first directly beneath Sentinel Dome, providing grand and unusual views into Yosemite Valley, over 3,000 feet below. One of the most memorable is the unobstructed view of the entire 2,400-foot drop of Yosemite Falls, directly across the canyon, an aspect of this waterfall unique to this position along the Valley's rim. We are climbing through a splendid forest of Red Fir (*Abies magnifica*), interspersed with the dominant shrubs of this region—manzanita, chinquapin and ceanothus. Occasional flashes of color are provided by lupines, paintbrush and arrowhead groundsel in stunning combinations of blue, red and yellow. In early summer, this is a favorable area for the dramatic red snow plants, sometimes in groups of several large specimens. Here and there, the ground-hugging Pine-Mat Manzanita (*Arctostaphylos nevadensis*) unfolds its clusters of small, snow-white flowers like tiny urns, giving the foreground a glittering appearance. In dry, sunny areas, the orange-gold of sulphur flower is prominent, contrasting well with the subdued grays of the granite landscape. The brilliant rose-red of mountain-pride is abundant, sprawling recklessly across rocky outcroppings along the rim.

In a little less than two miles from Glacier Point we cross Sentinel Creek at the very place where it reaches the rim of Yosemite Valley and leaps over the edge in the first of a series of vertical cascades, to meet the Valley floor 3,300 feet below. Along the creek above the waterfall, interspersed with thickets of willow, are stream-side gardens of shooting-stars, lupine, wild asters, mountain violets. It is always rewarding to stand at the top of one of Yosemite's waterfalls, looking down the descending torrent and being carried in fancy on the drifting comets of white water. Sentinel Fall provides a broad rocky overlook point where the temptation is strong to cancel the rest of the hike and remain here for the day, alone with one's thoughts.

A climb of about one mile through open forests of red fir, Lodgepole Pine (*Pinus contorta* ssp. *murrayana*), Jeffrey Pines (*Pinus jeffreyi*) and occasional Western White Pines (*Pinus monticola*) brings us to the junction of the spur trail to the Glacier Point Road at the Sentinel Dome trailhead. This is a region of sunny, gravelly slopes blossoming with their own varieties of plants which are adapted to bright sunlight and well-drained, dry locations. In early summer, one of the most characteristic is the Spreading Phlox (*Phlox diffusa*) which forms prominent mats of white (sometimes lilac or pink), five-petalled flowers. The leaves are short, almost needle-like in appearance and texture. This plant is widespread across the Park, from 4,500 to 11,000 feet, adding a touch of delicacy to an otherwise rugged setting. A hardy perennial, its low-growing green mats can be seen through most of the period when snow does not lie on the ground, although its season of bloom is from June to early August.

Other flowers characteristic of these dry locations, and to be seen near this trail junction, are: pussy paws, golden brodiaea (similar to the one found earlier in the Sierran foothills), white-flowered Mariposa lilies, low-growing varieties of shieldleaf, the rich yellow tones of groundsel which is so prominent at this elevation, and the dainty little Collinsia *(Collinsia torreyi* var. *wrightii)* which grows only 6 inches high but may form solid expanses of delicate sky-blue and white blossoms.

Turning to the west, the Pohono Trail begins a gentle descent to the awesome overlook at Taft Point, about a half-mile farther. Almost at once, we pass through the first of many small, moist meadows where the silence is broken only by the water-music of a tiny stream and the melody of bird songs. These meadows, each a jewel, are among the memorable features of the Pohono Trail and provide distinctive habitats for a whole series of moisture-seeking plants.

One of the more showy species is the Little Leopard Lily *(Lilium parvum)*—sometimes referred to as Alpine Lily—which blooms on 2- to 4-foot stalks as a bouquet of numerous orange-yellow flowers with maroon spots. These flowers, 1 to 2 inches long, are tubular in form with some recurving at the ends of the petals, generally raising their heads as though to permit easy appreciation of their beauty. They put in their first appearance in late June and continue to flower until early August. Look for them in moist locations from Yosemite Valley (sparingly) to 9,000 feet.

Contrasting with the orange-yellow of this lily is the bright gold of the arrowhead groundsel, deep blue lupines on tall stalks *(Lupinus latifolius* var. *columbianus)*, and showy heads of paintbrush. Wild Geranium or Cranesbill *(Geranium richardsonii)* is another typical plant of these moist locations, with rounded white or pink blossoms, strikingly veined in purple. Deer's Tongue *(Frasera speciosa)* will be seen occasionally at the edge of these meadows—tall stalks 3 to 5 feet high with numerous greenish-white, star-shaped flowers.

At Taft Point, 3,500 feet above Yosemite Valley, is a rocky outcrop where the habitat changes again. Here is a typical location for that lacy member of the rose family called Mousetails *(Ivesia santolinoides)*, because of the strange similarity of the leaves to the long slender tails of these little rodents. This plant has a branching net-work of slender stems ending in minute white flowers which appear to wave in the air without visible means of support. Near the sheer edge of the rim grows the handsome shrub called Cream Bush *(Holodiscus boursieri)*, with pointed racemes of small cream-white flowers forming dense shafts of bloom. Service-Berry *(Amelanchier pallida)*, with five-petalled white flowers in random clusters is a tall, many-branched shrub also to be seen in bloom in this area. At ground level, look for a small Monkey-flower *(Mimulus leptaleus)* in contrasting tones of red and yellow, carpeting open areas among the forest trees.

The view from Taft Point is one of the finest along the south rim and deserves a long look. All the central part of Yosemite Valley is within sight, and the great north wall displays its varied structure from El Capitan to North Dome in an unbroken sweep. Nearby are large vertical cracks in the rim, known as the Fissures, where ages of erosion have removed the granite along joint planes in the rock, leaving narrow crevices of astounding depth.

As the trail heads west from Taft Point, it makes a wide arc to the south to descend into and climb out of the upper valley of Bridalveil Creek. Here we lose contact for a while with the Valley's rim as we thread our way through a mixed forest of firs and pines. But there is much to see, for we are in a region pleasantly varied between inspiring forests, idyllic mountain meadows and songful streams. One of the charming plants to seek under the red firs is the little White-Veined Shinleaf *(Pyrola picta)*, whose favored habitat is the deep humus of the shaded forest floor. Typically, it grows 4 to 12 inches high with erect stems holding a cluster of greenish-white blossoms, like small bells whose clappers are the protruding styles of the flowers. Always, the leaves are in a basal rosette and are most attractive in themselves—deep green with prominent veinings of white. These rosettes are an appealing feature of the forest floor even before the flowers appear and after they have faded into the seed stage. Expect to find pyrola from late June to August, from 4,000 to 7,500 feet.

As we cross the several streams which drain the rim country and are in this region tributary to Bridalveil Creek, one of the frequently seen flowers is the Red Columbine *(Aquilegia formosa)*. Rather commonly found from 4,000 to 9,000 feet, it blooms from May to August as spring advances to higher elevations. The deep red-orange color of petals and spurs, combined with the bright yellow stamens which protrude boldly, form a rich tonal combination which has made the columbine a favorite wherever it grows. Nature has been generous in its supply of this lovely blossom, to the great pleasure of the hummingbirds who drink deeply of the nectar in the long spurs behind the petals. The plant itself often grows to a height of 3 to 4 feet where moisture is favorable, with leaves deeply and attractively lobed.

Along these streams, in the willow thickets and bog gardens, the Red Osier Dogwood or American Dogwood *(Cornus stolonifera)* grows lushly. Its bright purplish-red stems, 4 to 12 feet high, produce clusters of tiny 4-petalled flowers which form flat umbels of shimmering white on the shrub. Like its close relative, the tree-sized mountain dogwood, its leaves turn red in the fall, making one of the brightest colors in the autumnal landscape. In early spring, before the leaves develop, the lacquered appearance of its colorful stems and branches is a pleasing accent in the somber greens and grays of the forest.

The trail now twists through the tall trees, occasionally coming close to the rim providing dramatic and unusual views into Yosemite Valley, then skirting the edge of several jewel-like meadows—serene and untouched in their forest isolation. Here the moisture-loving plants which flower in July are to be found in abundance—whole congregations of midsummer's most distinguished residents. Tall shafts of corn lily, bright areas of yellow monkeyflower, the nodding heads of rose-lavender wild asters, clusters of tiny bluebells or languid ladies, the vivid gold of groundsel and the scarlet of paintbrush, royal purple tones of delphinium—all combine in a palette of unforgettable color against a setting of emerald green grasses and mosses. One of the more charming of these dwellers in the meadows is a plant related to columbine, the Meadow Rue *(Thalictrum fendleri)*, growing on stalks up to 3 feet high, with deeply-lobed compound leaves. The blossoms are especially interesting in their form, although their color differs little from that of the stems or the leaves themselves. Long stamens, faintly yellow, hang from the circle of 4 to 7 sepals, swaying in any slight breeze like a delicate fringe. This unusual plant has no true petals.

In these same wet meadows, tall shafts of Purple Monkshood *(Aconitum colum-*

bianum) stand regally at the edge of the forest or near willow thickets. The stems are 2 to 6 feet high, with deeply lobed leaves. The distinctively shaped blossoms, 1 inch across, have a striking resemblance to the traditional hood of a monk, covering the face of the flower with a dark purple, sombre color. The plant is said to be poisonous, and grazing animals avoid it.

About 2½ miles from Taft Point, our trail crosses Bridalveil Creek, a robust stream which flashes along a sloping, forested valley, singing its way through thickets of willow and dogwood with wildflowers thronging its banks, thriving in the cool dampness. A rustic bridge provides easy crossing, and nearby is an ideal place for lunch and perhaps a period of quiet contemplation of the unspoiled quality of this sanctuary. The beautiful stream is as yet unaware of its turbulent destiny, less than 2 miles distant, for at the Valley's rim it will plunge over the 600-foot cliff to form spectacular Bridalveil Fall, a creature of mist and rainbows.

Just beyond the creek crossing, a lateral trail may be taken to the south, intersecting the Glacier Point Road near the Bridalveil Creek Campground. This trail is only slightly more than 2 miles long, taking one over the wide grassy reaches of McGurk Meadow and through long expanses of lodgepole pine forest. It makes possible the termination of the Pohono Trail hike at approximately its halfway point, if time is not available for the entire distance. Or, alternatively, one can start at Bridalveil Creek Campground and walk the remainder of the trail to the west, finishing at the Wawona Tunnel, a total distance of 9½ miles.

As we pass the McGurk Meadow Trail junction, the main Pohono Trail ascends a gentle sandy slope which often holds a remarkable display of Scarlet Gilia *(Ipomopsis aggregata).* The scarlet hue will be noticed as a vivid mass before one is near enough to be aware of the individual plants. There are few other mountain flowers that can rival it in color intensity, while the structure of the blossom itself is of interest too. Growing on erect stems, 1 to 2 feet high, the bright flowers remind one of a sharply pointed star, trailing a comet-like tail which is the long tube from which the five petals explode. The red color is offset by a mottling of yellow along the slender petals, while from the center emerges a cluster of bristling stamens. Gilia leaves are rather distinctive in their form: 1 to 4 inches long, divided into several minute and very slender sections. Scarlet gilia is a flower of dry, sandy slopes and will be found from 6,000 to 9,000 feet blooming from late June to mid-August. Look for it also along the Tioga Road at about the 8,000-foot elevation, and occasionally beside the Glacier Point Road as well. There is a notable display on the old Glacier Point Road, between the Badger Pass ski area and Bridalveil Creek Campground, a road which is closed to automobiles now but still affords a fascinating hike.

Magnificent red fir forest, interspersed with flowering meadows and small streams of cold, sweet mountain water continue to make the trail a constant source of happy surprises as we climb slowly out of the valley of Bridalveil Creek. Where the humus under the red fir is especially deep, look for an attractive member of the orchid family, the Spotted Coralroot *(Corallorhiza maculata).* Its brown stems rise 8 to 24 inches from the forest floor, with leaves which are mere clasping, papery sheaths. The flower head consists of 12 to 15 individual blossoms, varying in tone from magenta to chartreuse, but with a white lower lip which is usually spotted with crimson. Although each flower is only ½ inch long, there is no mistaking its relationship to the orchid family, for there is a close resemblance—in miniature—to the cultivated species. This plant is similar to the snow plant in that it lacks chlorophyll and hence is incapable of producing its own food in the normal way through photosynthesis. Through the aid of fungi growing in its roots, decaying organic matter in the soil is broken down for food. Spotted coralroot is not a common flower, but it does occur intermittently in the areas of suitably deep humus. The Pohono Trail is one of the best places to find it; another good location is in the general area of Glacier Point or Sentinel Dome, where the red firs provide the habitat it seeks. It blooms in July and August.

Dewey Point, at about 2½ miles from the crossing of Bridalveil Creek, is an overlook where the hiker is tempted to linger indefinitely. The trail sign announces that this platform in the sky is 7,316 feet in elevation—about 3,300 feet above Yosemite Valley's floor. Directly across the great chasm looms the famous cliff of El Capitan, its entire facade and vast sloping crest in full view. The lower canyon of Bridalveil Creek, terminating in the waterfall, slashes into the south rim of Yosemite directly to the east, while the summit peaks of the High Sierra lift jagged edges against the farthest eastern horizon. At Dewey Point, one feels alone with the sky and the wind, almost a fellow creature with the white-throated swifts that dart constantly from the rim far out over the canyon like tiny feathered projectiles.

On this rocky buttress grows one of the typical plants of the dry slopes, the little Stonecrop *(Sedum obtusatum)*. Its stems are only 1 to 6 inches high, reddish in tone, arising from rosettes of fleshy leaves. The small flowers form clusters of lemon-yellow color, often fading to pink, ½ to ¾ inch long. The whole effect is that of a carpet of warm gold thrown across the rocks, like congealed sunshine.

Heading west from Dewey Point, the Pohono Trail begins its long descent to meet the Wawona Road. It remains fairly close to the rim for the next two miles, offering climactic views into Yosemite Valley at several places. Just before reaching the next major overlook at Crocker Point (7,090 feet elevation), we cross another of those delightful little streams. Its cold, clear water encourages a lush growth of ferns, willows, red osier dogwood, yellow monkeyflower, meadow rue, groundsel, thimbleberry. From Crocker Point—well worth a stop—there is a memorable view of the full drop of Bridalveil Fall. In late afternoon, its rainbow is especially vivid as seen from this overlook.

A half mile farther is Stanford Point (6,659 feet elevation); the view from here consists of the same elements admired from Crocker Point, yet in a different scenic arrangement. The forest is now becoming the dominant feature of the trail, with huge mature specimens of Red Fir *(Abies magnifica)*, Sugar Pine *(Pinus lambertiana)* and Jeffrey Pine *(Pinus jeffreyi)* making up much of the woodland. On the dark maroon trunks of the red fir, the contrasting chartreuse of the Staghorn Lichen *(Letharia vulpina)* is especially prominent. It grows on the ridges of the bark and on dead branches, forming fur-like coverlets, 2 inches or more in depth, that seem strikingly brilliant against the somber tones of the forest. This lichen is an epiphyte, or air plant, deriving its sustenance from air and sunlight while using the trees only as a means of support. It does no harm, as a parasite would, to the tree on which it grows.

The last of the major overlooks along the Pohono Trail is Old Inspiration Point (6,603 feet elevation). Although no trail leads down to the actual point itself from the Pohono, it is not difficult to scramble through the manzanita and chinquapin brush to the place where in 1851, according to history, the initial party of white men to enter Yosemite Valley (the Mariposa Battalion) beheld their first view of the canyon they had been seeking. Their actual descent from this point to the Valley floor was to the west, the route followed closely today by the Pohono Trail.

Now the trail drops relentlessly for the remaining 3 miles to the Wawona Road. The red firs are seen no more, preferring the higher reaches of the rim country; their place is taken by the White Fir *(Abies concolor)*. Their trunks are dark grey to silver, their crowns a bit more spire-like than those of red firs, yet the trees are of comparable size. No festoons of staghorn lichen decorate them, however. Ponderosa Pines *(Pinus ponderosa)* come into the forest community in increasing numbers as the trail continues its descent. They will be found all the way to Yosemite Valley, where they are the dominant conifer. Long golden beams of late afternoon sunshine reach through the forest aisles. Huge Black Oaks *(Quercus kelloggii)* join the pines and firs; they too will be present all the way to Yosemite Valley. Beneath these forest monarchs is an understory of shrubbery: manzanita, ceanothus (deer brush), azalea along moist water courses, rounded masses of Huckleberry Oaks *(Quercus vaccinifolia)*. Often one can hear in the distance, almost dream-like, the rhythmic hooting or drumming of the male dusky grouse, a low but resonant sound that vibrates through the forest. Occasionally, a startled deer bounds away through the trees. The serenity of a mountain evening lies across the land like a benediction at the close of a memorable day.

Inspiration Point, only a mile from the Wawona Road and 1,000 feet above the well-known Tunnel View on that road, is the last major scenic landmark along the Pohono Trail. Here, the trail crosses the original Wawona Road, opened in 1875, at the place where early travelers to Yosemite stopped for their first inspiring glimpse into the famous valley they had come so far to see. The view remains unchanged today, for the National Park Service has safeguarded it against despoilment by roads, buildings or other man-made additions to the landscape, all of which are effectively concealed on the Valley floor. There is little doubt that this viewpoint offers the most comprehensive of all Yosemite Valley vistas—from Bridalveil Meadow just below us to Cloud's Rest at the extreme eastern end of the canyon. This view always affords a mood of tranquility as well as inspiration, yet it is one which is seen by comparatively few visitors.

One mile down the trail brings us to the Wawona Road, where we will welcome the chance to rest after long miles on foot. The farsighted will have arranged for transportation from here. Weariness may be the predominant feeling of the moment, but the day has been one of enriching memories of far-flung vistas, of the inspiring architecture of great trees, of sparkling meadows and singing streams, of the sight and sound of birds, and especially of a panorama of wildflowers not often excelled. In Yosemite's rim country, the Pohono Trail is typical of the best of its widely varying flower habitats.

Deer Brush

Blue Penstemon

Alum-Root

Washington Lily

Mountain-Pride

California Coneflower

Lungwort or Mountain Bluebell

Sierra Rein Orchid

Pink Monkeyflower

Corn Lily

Camas Lily

Shooting Star

Scarlet Monkeyflower

Larkspur

Marsh Marigold

Arrowhead Groundsel

Yampah

Fireweed

44

Davidson's Fritillary

Sulphur Flower

Sierra Forget-Me-Not or Stickseed

Little Leopard Lily

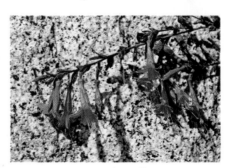

California Fuchsia

Spreading Phlox

45

White-Veined Shinleaf

Scarlet Gilia

Red Columbine

Pearly Everlasting

Spotted Coralroot

Meadow Rue

Wild Geranium

Cream Bush

Red Osier Dogwood or American Dogwood

Monkshood

Thimbleberry

Knotweed

47

THE SUBALPINE BELT
AND THE
HIGH SIERRA LOOP TRAIL

Just as in the month of July spring will have fully matured in Yosemite's rim country—between 6,000 and 8,000 feet—in August this magic season will move on up the mountain slopes to paint with color the meadows, lake shores and rocky ridges of the higher elevations. This region, just under tree line and with bare granite peaks etching jagged shapes against the sky, is known to its devotees simply as the "High Country."

Those who know it best will tell you that here the Sierra attains its ultimate perfection of mountain grandeur. Near the source of eternal snows on the peaks, icy streams flash down the mountain slopes to linger a while in the grassy meanders of lush meadows, trailing garlands of wildflowers along their banks. Many lakes, from the smallest of rocky tarns to those filling ancient glacial valleys, lie in grass-rimmed splendor reflecting the sky, the clouds and the crags. Alabaster-white granite, sometimes mottled with the rust of iron oxide, rises in sharp summits against the azure sky. The russet of metamorphic rock adds a contrast along some parts of the Sierran crest.

Throughout this whole landscape is an infinity of exquisite rock gardens—ledges and tiny meadows of mosses, grasses, flowers and wind-sculptured trees. Each one is different, each one is a delight to encounter. Watered by occasional summer showers and the residue of winter moisture, these are the places where spring's last blooms appear before the approach of autumn. At this elevation the growing season is only 7 to 9 weeks between winter and fall, so the pace is furious and often one finds many species in bloom simultaneously. Even on the mountain tops, from 12,000 to 13,000 feet, spring's influence is felt; about 170 different types of flowering plants including grasses and sedges have been classified in the Alpine Zone, above tree line. We will find a few of them in the next chapter.

Tuolumne Meadows—Lemmon's Paintbrush

One of the easiest ways to sample the unforgettable beauty of the High Country is to drive the Tioga Road all the way to the Park's eastern gateway at 9,941-foot Tioga Pass. Near the roadsides many of the typical flowers to be described in this chapter will be found, especially if short excursions are made on foot from the scenic viewpoints provided along the route.

Tuolumne Meadows, 8,600 feet in elevation, is an excellent place to explore; during July and August an impressive number of the flowers in this mountain region can be found in and near this beautiful area. By continuing beyond Tioga Pass, down the scenic Lee Vining Canyon grade to Mono Lake (only an additional 15 miles), one gets a selection of those somewhat different species growing in the drier environment on the east side of the Sierra—facing the arid region of the Great Basin and the sagebrush belt.

However, by far the best way to establish an intimate acquaintance with the flowering residents of Yosemite's High Country is to travel some of the trails which radiate like the spokes of a wheel from Tuolumne Meadows. Trails to beauty may be long or short, depending almost entirely on your time, interest and energy; they may require only two hours or can occupy two weeks or more.

The best known trail is the High Sierra Loop, starting from Tuolumne Meadows Lodge and tying together the five High Sierra Camps which operate from early July until Labor Day. These camps offer meals and lodgings in rustic tent accommodations, each one in a different setting which thus runs the gamut of High Sierra scenery. Advance reservations are very essential, because of the small size of the camps and their popularity; these arrangements can be made by writing or phoning the Reservations Office of the Yosemite Park and Curry Co., in Yosemite National Park. The five camps are spaced along the trail at intervals of about 8 miles, the entire Loop aggregating approximately 50 miles. Many people walk or ride on mules around this Loop each summer, but if time is not available for the entire trail even a day's hike to one of the camps can be rewarding. National Park Service naturalists accompany the once-a-week scheduled Seven Day Hikes.

Let's take a walk on the High Sierra Loop Trail and find some of the many flowers which live there. The Loop can be walked in either direction, but the route used most often runs north from Tuolumne Meadows to the first High Camp at Glen Aulin, returning finally to the point of origin via Vogelsang Camp. Going this way, one has an easy first day on the trail, mostly downhill for about 6 miles, in which to get accustomed to the demands of higher altitude on one's energy supply.

Crossing Tuolumne Meadows itself, there will be an opportunity to become acquainted with a number of the flowers which will be seen again and again on this trail. One which often appears in massed colonies, making splashes of magenta across the wide green floor of the meadow, is Lemmon's Paintbrush (Castilleja lemmonii), perhaps the brightest of all this large genus of mountain flowers. Its vividly colored blossoms are lifted 4 to 8 inches high on slender stems which grow as a small group from a single root stalk, with linear leaves 1 or 2 inches long. The actual flower of the paintbrush is an elongated tube, but many are crowded into a dense terminal spike interspersed with purplish or magenta bracts. The total effect is of a burst of floral color on a short stem, often barely higher than the surrounding grass. This paintbrush is easily mistaken for Owl's Clover (Orthocarpus purpurascens) which, however, rarely occurs above 5,000 feet and never reaches the High Country.

Another flower commonly seen in Tuolumne Meadows is a little Buttercup (Ranunculus alismaefolius var. alismellus). Look for it in damp places, where its 6- to 12-inch stems bear bright yellow, 5-petalled blossoms, a half an inch across. The waxy shine of its petals will distinguish this little flower from other yellow ones which seem to have a superficial resemblance to it. Buttercups are one of the first flowers of springtime, so are more usually seen in the High Country in June and July, though some will remain in bloom into August. If one drives the Tioga Road about the first of July, another early bloomer to be seen in Tuolumne Meadows is the Pigmy Shooting Star (Dodecatheon jeffreyi ssp. pygmaeum). A variation on the one seen in the wet meadows of lower elevations, this one makes bold magenta-pink splashes of color as the first green returns to the meadow turf, even though its stems are only 3 to 8 inches high.

An attractive small aster ranges widely over the meadows in July and August (Aster alpigenus ssp. andersonii). It grows as a single pink blossom, an inch or more across, on the tip of a slender stem only a few inches high; only one flower is allotted to each plant. Its leaves are so slender they appear to be mere blades of grass in the broad sweep of the meadow. Often, it will be found intermingled with Lemmon's paintbrush, the two producing a most pleasing color variation from pink to magenta.

Near the Soda Springs, where heavily impregnated mineral water bubbles up continuously from a reddish-tinged bank, is a stand of Deer's Tongue (Frasera speciosa). This large, rather coarse plant is easy to recognize with its 3- to 5-foot high stalks and its graceful whorls of 3 to 7 leaves. The latter are long—4 to 10 inches— covered with tiny, soft hairs and remind one of the out-thrust tongue of a deer. The flowers are a striking geometric pattern, arranged in fours (4 petals, 4 sepals, 4 stamens), about an inch across and greenish-white in color. This huge plant is in the gentian family, sometimes called Green Gentian; we will encounter some very different and smaller species farther along the trail.

Commonly seen across Tuolumne Meadows, too, is the Whorled Penstemon (*Penstemon oreocharis*), growing typically on slender stems 8 to 20 inches high. Each stalk supports 1 to 6 whorls of blue-purple tubular flowers, a half inch long, which contrast pleasingly with the yellowing meadow grasses of late summer.

Almost reluctantly, we leave Tuolumne Meadows, the largest area of grassland in the High Sierra, to begin the trek around the Loop Trail. However, it does promise an unending variety of visual delights for as long as we have time to savor them. From the Soda Springs we have an easy segment of the trail, little more than 5 miles, to our first objective, Glen Aulin High Sierra Camp. The route leads through a picturesque forest of lodgepole pines, past miniature meadows of grass and sedge, across open flats where vistas of distant peaks and domes loom in every direction. Within a mile we will cross a delightful stream, Delaney Creek, one of many we will encounter on this trail. Beyond it, in the open flat before we cross Dingley Creek, is a warm dry area ideal for the growth of a plant which prefers such a Spartan habitat: the odd little Mousetails (*Ivesia santolinoides*), which we met along the Pohono Trail.

After crossing Dingley Creek, we follow close by the Tuolumne River for some time, enjoying wide views of the rugged Cathedral Group of peaks and crags to the south. In early summer, snow lies deeply in the cirques of their north-facing slopes; the blue water of the river and the deep green of the meadow grasses contrast dramatically with their wintry aspect. Just ahead is an expanse of meadow, surrounded by lodgepole pines, which often exhibits a fine showing of flower color: the flame of Lemmon's paintbrush; pink shooting stars; the silvery sheen of Pussytoes (*Antennaria rosea*), tiny silken heads scattered far and wide over the meadows; the first brightness of alpine goldenrod; deep purple whorled penstemons. Such mosaics of color are one of the memorable rewards of High Sierra hiking.

Now, our trail leaves the gentleness of meadowy landscapes, threads its way over rocky domes, and crosses the now-turbulent Tuolumne on a picturesque footbridge. From this point, we make a continuous descent toward Glen Aulin, following the river closely, a roaring torrent of white water most of the way. Less than a mile above Glen Aulin, the river plunges over a sheer drop exceeding a hundred feet, forming Tuolumne Fall, the first of five spectacular waterfalls in this area.

Shortly above the waterfall and along the trail is a fine display of Labrador-Tea (*Ledum glandulosum* var. *californicum*). These are rather stiffly branched shrubs, 1 to 5 feet high with leathery, deep green leaves up to 2 inches long. The leaves exude a pleasant fragrance not unlike that of turpentine. In midsummer, the shrubs bear masses of white flowers, individually tiny but forming compact heads 3 to 4 inches across. You will find this attractive shrub in damp areas or around lakeshores.

Just before reaching the Camp, we come to the top of the White Cascade, where the Tuolumne flings itself tumultuously over a high granite bench into a deep green pool. Because of the ever-present moisture from the mist, this region is a favored one for several of the most beautiful High Country flowers.

The bright gold of Arnica (*Arnica nevadensis*) seems to take its color from the very sunlight. In the sunflower family, its flowers are 2 inches wide and look not unlike the common sunflower itself. The stems are $\frac{1}{2}$ to 2 feet high, with leaves mostly in pairs, frequently heart-shaped, woolly and somewhat aromatic.

For contrast, the Mountain Daisy *(Erigeron peregrinus)* blooms in shades of rose-purple with yellow centers, growing on stalks 4 to 20 inches high with long, slender leaves. Its flower heads are up to 2 inches wide and are usually solitary on each stalk, even though a large number may be found growing together and giving the illusion of many-flowered plants. We will have this lovely flower as a trail-side companion frequently.

A strange little plant common along this trail will be seen here—the Shieldleaf *(Streptanthus tortuosus* var. *orbiculatus)*. It prefers rocky locations and finds them in the massive granite near the waterfall. Round leaves clasp the slender stems, which may be $1/2$ to $1^1/2$ feet high. Green in early summer, the leaves later turn gold, resembling circular brass shields. At the tips of the stems the small purple flowers (sometimes whitish) occur in a raceme of several. They resemble tiny urns, about $1/2$ inch long. In the seed stage, long slender pods are produced, like miniature string beans. These long pods, and the prominent yellow leaves, make the plant easy to recognize.

Others adding their beauty to this rock garden by the White Cascade are: Golden Stars *(Brodiaea gracilis)*, with 5-pointed yellow petals and brown mid-veins; tall stalks of yellow senecio similar to those encountered in the rim country; deep blue spikes of lupine; the royal purple of larkspur; white yarrow, its flat clusters of tiny flowers making highlights in the forest shadows; the ever-present, delicate pussytoes; the crimson tones of mountain-pride penstemon; the lemon-yellow of Stonecrop *(Sedum obtusatum)*, with small clusters of flowers and thick fleshy leaves which often turn faintly pink, creeping over rocky crevices.

A half mile below the High Sierra Camp is the Glen Aulin itself, from which the Camp takes its name. Here, the river seems to rest for a while, drifting slowly through a thick stand of aspen, fir and pine, its quiet surface mirroring the clouds and the forest. It is a place for peaceful contemplation, a quiet grotto, seemingly far removed from the turbulence of the river just above and below the Glen. Beyond it, to the west, the Tuolumne continues its downward plunge toward its eventual destiny in Hetch Hetchy Reservoir. Along the way, it forms California Falls, then LeConte Falls. Three miles from Glen Aulin Camp is one of the most impressive white water spectacles in all of Yosemite National Park—the Waterwheel Falls. Best seen in early summer when the water is high, it features great vertical "wheels" of spray, created when the swift river plunges over upcurving spoons of granite, along a mile of its course. Many of the flowers we have admired on our walk from Tuolumne Meadows can be seen in this area too and, if time is available, the 7-mile round-trip detour to the Waterwheels will provide a memorable experience. However, the High Sierra Loop Trail leads elsewhere.

Our trail turns to the west, toward May Lake High Sierra Camp, about opposite the top of the White Cascade. Now we will do a little climbing, for May Lake is some 1,500 feet higher than Glen Aulin and $8^1/2$ miles distant. Within less than a mile we come to McGee Lake, an idyllic place where the calm water is enclosed by deep lodgepole pine forest, leaving open windows through the trees at either end, however, for inspiring views of Mt. Conness (12,590 feet) to the east and Mt. Hoffmann (10,921 feet) to the west. Though we may only have started our hike for the day at this point, the urge to pause for a while amid such serenity is nearly irresistible.

Shortly thereafter, the trail crosses Cathedral Creek, a robust stream at times, which rises under Cathedral Peak and flows northward to join the Tuolumne River several miles west of Waterwheel Falls. In this region, notice the infiltration of Mountain Hemlock *(Tsuga mertensiana)*, one of the most beautiful trees of the Sierran forests and one which is mainly confined to the subalpine zone. Larger, mature specimens are characterized by richly cinnamon-colored trunks and dark green foliage, with small, cylindrical cones, 3 inches long. Young trees are extremely slender and graceful in appearance, their tops often drooping slightly, with a limber quality unknown to most pines which stand with them in the forest aisles. Their blue-green needles cluster thickly on the branches, producing almost a fern-like quality.

Another handsome tree of these elevations, now appearing here and there along the trail, is the Western White Pine *(Pinus monticola)*, also called Silver Pine. With needles in groups of five, it is closely related to the much larger sugar pine. Its cones are similarly long and cylindrical but much smaller (4 to 8 inches) than the huge cones of sugar pines.

Our trail continues to climb, and not long after passing the junction of the Ten Lakes Trail, we cross a prominent granite spur which affords the most sweeping view of the entire day's walk between Glen Aulin and May Lake. Mt. Conness and the adjacent peaks of the Sierran crest loom against the horizon to the east. Lembert Dome, towering above Tuolumne Meadows, can be seen clearly while, to the south, Tenaya Lake sparkles in the sunlight, nestled in a basin of huge domes.

On this portion of the trail, we pass again some of those incredible rock gardens of the High Sierra. Where small streams descend from higher sources of snow melt, the rose-purple blooms of Spiraea *(Spiraea densiflora)* offer dramatic contrast to the white granite rocks. This member of the rose family grows as a low bush, 3 to 5 feet high, with small dentate leaves resembling those of roses. The prominent flowers, individually tiny, occur in flat-topped clusters which give the appearance of single blossoms 2 inches wide. A patchwork quilt of other flower colors enlivens these gardens too: the bright red of mountain-pride; tall spikes of purplish lupine; deep sky-blue of Sierra forget-me-not; tall stalks of red-orange paintbrush; dark purple larkspur; the startling white of yarrow's flat-topped heads; the distinctive rounded, yellow leaves and purple flowers of shieldleaf. If one looks closely at these damp stream-side gardens, the muted blue flowers of Speedwell *(Veronica alpina var. alterniflora)* will be seen among the grasses and sedges. The tiny flower is less than $1/2$ inch wide, 4-petalled, and appears as a short raceme on erect stems 4 to 12 inches high with leaves in pairs.

Just below the ridge lies little Raisin Lake, a favorite of fishermen. Surrounding it is a heavy growth of Labrador-Tea. Nearby are some small meadows, lush with the dampness which drains into the lake, a classical habitat for flowers which prefer marshy conditions. Here again are asters, buttercups, lupines, tall senecios and the corn lily, found in the meadows of the rim country. A tiny stream trickles across granite pavement and nearby are fine showings of the Pink Monkeyflower *(Mimulus lewisii)*. In any rating of all the flowers of Yosemite, this one would have to rank near the top in exquisite beauty.

Beyond this meadowy region, our trail climbs again, up and up to the final ridge enclosing May Lake. From the top, another sweeping panorama of High Sierran peaks unfolds: Mt. Clark's sharp pinnacle (11,522 feet) to the south, Tenaya Peak (10,301 feet) above Tenaya Lake, the Gothic-appearing architecture of Cathedral Peak (10,940 feet) in the east near Tuolumne Meadows, Mt. Conness on the far north-eastern horizon, with many more bare domes and ridges rimming our vista. On this rocky promontory, another gravel garden is provided for our pleasure by the plants of the dry environments: pink pussy paws; richly red mountain-pride; warm-toned golden stars; small purple blossoms of shieldleaf; the yellow-gray Alpine Paintbrush (Castilleja nana), only 3 inches high, crouching among the rocks; mats of pink and white phlox creeping across the gravelly slope.

And so, on down to May Lake and its High Sierra Camp, situated under the east face of Mt. Hoffmann. On its shores grows one of the most typical plants of these elevations, the Mountain Heather (Phyllodoce breweri). The flowers are rose-red, about ¹/₃ inch long, cup-shaped and with protruding stamens. They appear in terminal clusters on the rather short stems (6 to 12 inches), which are crowded with many small narrow leaves resembling fir needles. The impression is of a miniature forest of firs, as these shrubs hug the ground in their stiff manner of growth. Although most of the blossoms appear in early summer, the pervasive green of the shrubs themselves is one of the most common features of the flora of the subalpine zone. Growing prominently with the heather around May Lake is much Labrador-Tea.

This area is difficult to leave. Mt. Hoffmann beckons the hiker, for an easy route leads to its summit and the view extends to the far horizon in every direction. The peak is located in almost the geographic center of Yosemite National Park, overlooking a vast wilderness panorama. A beautiful meadow nestles under the peak, near the route to the summit, where a fine stand of pink mimulus and other flowers of wet locations can be enjoyed.

Leaving the May Lake area our trail begins a sharp descent of about 1,100 feet to Tenaya Lake. Along the upper part of this trail we pass some magnificent specimens of western white pine. The flowers follow us, too, most generally those of the dry locations: shieldleaf, mountain-pride, phlox, paintbrush. Pine-Mat Manzanita (Arctostaphylos nevadensis) can be seen near the trail, bearing a strong resemblance to the much larger type we observed in the foothill region below the park. However, the pure white blossoms rather than pink ones, and the ground-hugging propensities of this species, clearly distinguish it.

About a mile below May Lake we reach a portion of the old Tioga Road which was left intact to furnish access to this trail junction when the present road realignment was completed in 1961. Hikers going into the northern part of Yosemite National Park find it convenient to drive to this point and start their trip here. A small pool, the residue of nearby snow melt, forms here in early summer, providing the moisture for a fine display of Jeffrey shooting star. Mountain heather adds its bit to the beauty of the area, too.

From this point, our trail follows the old Tioga Road for another mile to Tenaya Lake. This portion has been closed to traffic since the new road was built, so it has become a most scenic element of the trail system. Particularly fine views of the Tenaya Lake basin are enjoyed as we descend, while due south we see Mt. Clark as a sharp spire on the horizon. Many of the flowers we have found since starting our trip at Tuolumne Meadows will be seen again along this old road, which traverses areas of forest, of tiny meadows and of open rocky slopes as it descends.

From Tenaya Lake, there is a choice of routes leading on to Sunrise High Sierra Camp, which is situated at the lower end of Long Meadow. The shorter trail (about 5 miles) climbs a steep series of switchbacks to Forsythe Pass, then turns east to thread its way past the three Sunrise Lakes, over a divide north of Sunrise Mountain and down to the High Sierra Camp.

The other trail is longer (8 miles) but infinitely rewarding in the spectacular quality of its scenery and wealth of flowers. In 1963, Mary Tresidder took a trip around this portion of the High Sierra Loop Trail, to Sunrise, Merced Lake and Vogelsang Camps. As a by-product of this outing, she compiled a detailed check-list of plants in bloom at that time, a sort of floral diary of an enriching experience. With this as a handbook, we will follow the longer trail to Sunrise Camp via Cathedral Pass.

To reach the beginning, we turn east at Tenaya Lake toward Tuolumne Meadows —an additional distance of 7 miles through a landscape of huge gray domes, tall lodgepole pines and occasional gleaming meadows. The present Tioga Road parallels this part of the trail; a choice of driving or walking is thus open. If time is available, though, the trail is well worth the walking. Our alternate trail to Sunrise Camp is reached soon after our arrival in Tuolumne Meadows, where Budd Creek crosses the Tioga Road.

Leaving Tuolumne, the trail immediately starts to climb toward Cathedral Peak, through a heavy forest of lodgepole pine, hemlock, western white pine and occasional red firs. Within less than a mile, we reach the first of several level benches on the north side of the Peak. Some of these are dry, but others are the sites of damp meadows providing flower gardens of rich variety. Lavender asters, deeply purple lupines, tall stalks of corn lilies, marsh marigolds, glossy little buttercups, mountain heather, pussytoes make a happy company in these forest glades.

A tiny plant, almost unnoticed, forms an extensive part of the ground cover of these subalpine meadows. This is Dwarf Bilberry (Vaccinium nivictum), growing recumbent on the turf, its smoothly rounded branchlets only 1 to 3 inches high, with shiny green, alternate leaves. The small pink or white urn-shaped flowers, less than ¼ inch long, bloom in early summer and produce blue-black berries. Often one sees it creeping across granite rocks at the edge of a meadow, its tiny head not more than an inch or two above the ground. In September, the leaves of the little plant turn a vivid crimson, making a striking contrast to the gold of the meadow grasses.

Along drier parts of the trail, look for the shimmering yellow of Wallflower (Erysimum perenne). Its flowers, with four, almost-round petals, are less than an inch across but they bloom as a curved head or elongated spike of color on stiff stalks 8 to 24 inches high. Wallflower is in the mustard family, as is the shieldleaf, and the seed pods of each are quite long and slender, forming while individual blossoms farther up the stem are yet in flower. These distinctive pods make each plant easy to recognize. One of the memorable qualities of this wallflower is the pleasantly sweet fragrance it exudes, but one must bend low to savor it.

Other dwellers in the dry flats or in sunny areas between the tall pines and firs are: the yellow globes of sulphur flower; a low-growing groundsel or senecio, also bright yellow; the little white stars of phlox; crimson mountain-pride. As the trail climbs closer to the north side of Cathedral Peak, we enter a fine forest of hemlock, enjoying the darkly fluted cinnamon-colored trunks of the mature trees and the equally attractive grace of the young ones, clothed in blue-green needles. Farther along, a delightfully open meadow rimmed with Aspen trees (Populus tremuloides) provides an excellent vista of Fairview Dome, to the north. A small stream picks its way leisurely through the grass, providing the moisture so desired by the aspens.

This region, in the large cirque just north of Cathedral Peak, is well supplied with water from the snowfields which lie in the deep shadow of the north wall and remain as snow late into the summer. Evidences of winter avalanches can be seen, where great snowslides have carved gashes through the forest. About two miles after leaving Tuolumne Meadows, conveniently located on a steep portion of our trail, is a most welcome spring of clear mountain water. The stream which flows from it nourishes a fine display of mountain heather, marsh marigold, Labrador-Tea, lupine.

A smaller flower, frequently seen in moist habitats such as along these streams and in wet meadows of the High Country, is the Meadow Monkeyflower *(Mimulus primuloides)*. The scientific name gives a clue to its appearance for it means, literally, primrose-like. The small yellow blossom, less than an inch wide, does in fact remind one of a primrose. It rises on short stems from a cluster of hairy leaves, presenting a round, golden face, funnelform with a drooping lower lip and a scattering of red-brown spots across the lower petals.

Rounding the north face of Cathedral Peak, we approach Upper Cathedral Lake, lying in a little basin with meadowy lawns sloping down on all sides. A small tributary stream crosses our route, providing moisture for an interesting growth of arnica, lupines, asters, senecios. The meadow itself is covered with the bright flames of Lemmon's paintbrush, the yellow of goldenrod, blue-purple lupines, delicately pink Anderson's asters. We have a sublime view of the great south face of Cathedral Peak with its twin turrets, as we look back across the lake. To the east, the sharp pinnacles of the Echo Peaks form an exciting horizon, while to the south Tresidder Peak (named for Dr. Donald Tresidder, former president of Stanford University and husband of Mary Tresidder) juts into the sky. This is a place of unusual, soul-satisfying beauty— one which is difficult to leave.

An easy climb brings us to the top of nearby Cathedral Pass, highest point on the trail to Sunrise High Sierra Camp. Here the view is more extensive and includes the peaks surrounding Matterhorn Canyon in the far northern reaches of Yosemite National Park and, in the other direction, the sharp crest of the Clark Range near the southern boundary. A marshy meadow extends for some distance after we cross the pass, the trail skirting it on the west under the rocky talus slopes of Tresidder Peak. Ahead, looms the sharp spire of Columbia Finger, and the trail heads for a gap which takes us close under the sheer side of this unusual landmark. The small blonde Alpine Paintbrush *(Castilleja nana)* will be seen growing in the gravels nearby. Much of the rock here shows the prominence of feldspar phenocrysts imbedded in its structure— strange little cubes of granite scattered in random fashion within the rocks or weath-ered out, to make piles of small blocks an inch or more square.

On a ridge east of the trail as it curves around Columbia Finger is an interesting and attractive plant, Lobb's Buckwheat *(Eriogonum lobbii)*. It prefers exposed rocky ridges, and crouches on the granite, sending out slender stems from a basal rosette of woolly, gray leaves. These stems too lie flat on the rock surface, as though weighted down by the large, round flower heads of white to rose. The heads are composed of many minute flowers which crowd together to give the appearance of a single globe of color, extremely appealing in its contrast to the clean, gray granite. You can find it commonly in similar situations on exposed rocky ridges at 8,000 to 9,000 feet.

In the same general area, look for the pink tone of pussy paws in the gravelly crevices. Another plant typical of these locations is also to be seen here: the little Sandwort *(Arenaria kingii)*. Its tiny white flowers have 5 petals on very slender stems, 4 to 8 inches high, from mostly basal leaves which are needle-like in structure and somewhat bristly. The presence of this delicate flower in such a rugged granite setting seems remarkable.

Now our trail drops steadily into the upper end of Long Meadow, descending from the broken granite landscape of the last mile into the lush greenness of a stream-watered valley. Occasionally, deer interrupt their browsing to disappear into the forest as we pass. Gradually, the lodgepole pines and willows give way to expansive meadows where our old friends of the trail—asters, paintbrush, goldenrod, dwarf bilberry, lupine—luxuriate in the mellowness of late afternoon.

Sunrise Camp, at an elevation of 9,300 feet, is situated on a grassy bench near the lower end of the meadow with a wide view in three directions—north toward Columbia Finger, the Echo Peaks, Tresidder Peak, Cathedral Peak and the great granite ridge of Matthes Crest, a mile long and almost 2,000 feet above its base—east toward the Sierran crest, where Mt. Florence dominates the scene at 12,561 feet—south to the sharp horn of Mt. Clark. The large expanse of green in the foreground gives an aspect of serenity to the scene. To the west is a high ridge over which lie the three Sunrise Lakes, an hour from Camp. Down this side comes a musical stream which flows through the Camp area, across the meadow and on to join Echo Creek.

Such a setting promotes a fine growth of wildflowers, and one is not likely to be disappointed with the Sunrise displays. Again, we will meet the shiny yellow butter-cups; the dwarf bilberry; the rose red of spiraea; sky-blue Sierra forget-me-nots; deeply purple whorled penstemons; primly white yarrow; lavender and gold asters; crimson paintbrush; golden senecio. They form a brilliant company, inhabiting the moist meadow and stream-side locations. Clambering over rocks or basking in sunny, gravelly areas, one often finds the yellow sulphur flower; magenta-toned mountain-pride penstemon; lavender stars of phlox; rosy bells of mountain heather; pink pussy paws.

Other attractions may vie for our interest in this beautiful area. Strange little "picket pins" (Belding ground squirrels) scamper across the meadow grass, stand stiffly erect while appraising our moves and then, with a shrill whistle, disappear from sight. Another ground squirrel, the golden-mantle, is often seen near Camp, scurrying here and there in his ceaseless quest for food. Sometimes, we may be fortunate enough to see a Sierra marmot sunning himself on a rock. This large (14 to 18 inches) relative of the woodchuck is a mellow gold in tone, has a large tail, and is reasonably common at these elevations. Little gray chickadees, with black-striped heads, forage through the pines for insects. Mountain bluebirds hover over the meadow or perch on rocks or small trees, scanning the area for insect food. Their horizon-blue color has about it the quality of a wildflower.

Mary Tresidder had a special love for Sunrise Camp, as she and her husband often had camped on the very ledge where it now is located. Feeling that there was such a unique quality to the place that she wanted to share it with other lovers of the High Country, she contributed a substantial part of the cost of its construction. A bronze plaque, inconspicuously located in a huge rock, commemorates her gener-osity and intimate association with this superb region.

The trail to Merced Lake and its High Sierra Camp crosses Long Meadow and works its way into the valley of Echo Creek, first following its Cathedral Fork for several miles to its junction with the main stream. The valley becomes deep, and for periods we seem to lose contact with the impressive mountains around us. From time to time, we can look up side canyons to remote peaks in the east. There is much to engage our attention, though, in the wildflowers along this fine stream. As we gradually lose elevation (Merced Lake is 7,275 feet above sea level) we find some of our old friends from the rim country reappearing, together with those we have come to know on the present trip.

Deep blue larkspurs, pink shooting stars, richly orange leopard lilies, sky-blue forget-me-nots, tall Indian paintbrush, yellow sulphur flowers, lavender asters, white yarrow, orange-gold senecio, mountain phlox—all are similar to those we admired in the rim country gardens, yet there are many we have learned to know in the last few days, too. Gooseberries *(Ribes montigenum)* are encountered along the creek; their red fruit is ripe in August and makes a tempting but tart trailside snack.

We continue to descend as the trail follows the creek, finally dropping into Echo Valley where we meet the main Merced River, less than two miles below Merced Lake itself.

Near the lower end of the trail along Echo Creek, look for a common plant of the dry locations in medium elevations—the Mountain Pennyroyal *(Monardella odoratissima)*. It is multi-branched, with straight stems to about a foot high, bearing flat clusters of pale lavender flowers, fading to gray, about an inch across. Since it is a mint, the leaves are in pairs while the stems are often 4-sided. The aromatic leaves, when rubbed between the fingers, give off a strong mint fragrance which is pleasant and makes a tasty cup of tea. You will find it frequently along the trail in dry areas of good drainage.

As we approach Merced Lake, many of the flowers of the Rim Country meet us once more: the fragrance of wild azalea (in July—faded by August), huge umbels of cream-colored cow parsnip, brilliant orange leopard lilies, tall white stalks of corn lilies, pink pussy paws, the rose-like white blossoms of wild strawberries, golden senecio. Much aspen grows in this part of the Merced Canyon, its round leaves on fragile stems glittering as the afternoon breeze moves through the groves.

The Camp lies in a picturesque setting at the east end of the lake, surrounded by a luxuriant forest of Jeffrey pine, lodgepole pine and white fir. The high peaks stand farther back and are not easily seen without going out on the trails. However this is just what should be done; there is much to see, to discover, to enjoy in this region.

About three miles above Merced Lake, on the upper reaches of the Merced River, is Washburn Lake, almost as large, with fine meadows extending yet farther up the canyon. Sparkling, singing streams of snow-melt come down from the high peaks of the Clark Range to the west and from the great basin under Mt. Lyell on the east, to form the headwaters of the Merced. This area was also a great favorite of Mary Tresidder; she and her husband often camped on these streams above Washburn Lake. As might be expected, wildflowers are in great numbers in these meadows and stream-side habitats, and many we have met before are here again to greet us: red columbines, orange leopard lilies, bright yellow monkeyflowers, tall golden senecios, crimson mountain-pride.

A striking yellow flower of the drier wooded slopes and forest openings is Mule-Ears *(Wyethia mollis)*. The large blossom, 1½ inches across, is similar to a sunflower, with 5 to 9 bright golden rays. Perhaps its most unusual feature, however, is the leaf structure, which gives the plant its name. Indeed, these huge leaves do look like mule ears, 8 to 16 inches long, woolly in texture and on stems which rise 1 to 3 feet. It grows frequently in the sunny north side of Tuolumne Meadows, also.

A charming flower of the trail-side, which we probably have noticed before, is the Mariposa Lily *(Calochortus leichtlinii)*. Its 3 snow-white petals, a dark purple spot at the base of each, form a softly moulded 2-inch-wide cup lifted on slender grass-like stems, 8 to 16 inches high. The narrow, basal leaves die back early, giving the flower the appearance of floating airily with little support. It prefers only gravelly locations; expect to see it often at these elevations. Mariposa is the Spanish word for butterfly; the flower's fancied resemblance to these beautiful winged creatures suggested the name. The roasted bulbs were an important part of the diet of Yosemite's Indians and other western tribes.

Between Merced Lake and Vogelsang High Sierra Camps there is again a choice of trails. One of them goes up Lewis Creek and over 10,700-foot Vogelsang Pass, a distance of 8½ miles. The other follows Fletcher Creek, gradually ascending toward the 10,160-foot elevation of Vogelsang Camp itself (without climbing the additional 500 feet to surmount the Pass). This trail is about one mile shorter. There is much to be enjoyed on either route, and each offers excellent summer wildflower gardens of the High Sierra. The dramatic view from Vogelsang Pass, highest point on the Loop Trail, includes unusual vistas of many high peaks along the Sierran crest, with rugged canyons and lake basins lying between them. On the other hand, the Fletcher Creek Trail follows near plunging cascades, great granite domes and lovely open meadows —with more intimate landscapes. It seems to have been a favorite of Mary Tresidder's, so let's take it this time.

One of the bright flowers seen frequently along this trail is the Cinquefoil *(Potentilla gracilis* ssp. *nuttallii)*. This little member of the rose family has 5 sunshine-gold petals, forming a shallow cup about an inch across, on stems ½ to 3 feet high. The compound leaves are interesting in themselves; they have 5 to 7 serrated leaflets arranged in a whorl radiating from the long leaf stem. The word "cinquefoil" means literally "five leaves," which refers to this type of leaf arrangement. Potentillas are widespread throughout the Sierra, some with yellow flowers and some with white, but only those with the digitate leaves, as in this species, are properly referred to as cinquefoils.

In the higher meadows, as our trail approaches Vogelsang Camp, we find a most attractive Lupine *(Lupinus covillei)*, "the beautiful silver foliage one," as Mary Tresidder described it. This member of the very large lupine genus (over 150 species, subspecies and varieties have been classified in California) occurs in the subalpine zone between 8,500 and 10,000 feet; the area we are traveling on this portion of the Loop Trail is a most typical habitat. The plant grows on tall straight stems, 1 to 2½ feet high, covered with soft, silky hairs. The leaves too are softly hairy, and in normal lupine fashion are composed of 7 to 9 long, slender leaflets. Tall racemes of deep blue flowers rise like a fringe above the mass of leaves, topped by the silvery caps of unopened buds. Thin, rocky soil of High Country meadows and the margins of tiny streams are the places it prefers.

The lower Fletcher Meadow, under Vogelsang Camp, is one of the most idyllic areas on this portion of the trail. The expansive views of craggy peaks above tree line,

59

the lawn-like meadow for a foreground, the icy clarity of Fletcher Creek, the seeming closeness to the blue Sierran sky, all contribute to a quality of serenity and remoteness long to be remembered happily by anyone fortunate enough to pass this way. As might be expected, many of the flowers we have come to know on this trip are represented in generous measure in the Fletcher Creek gardens: mountain-pride penstemon, spiraea, paintbrush, lavender asters, wallflowers, pussy paws, whorled penstemons, forget-me-nots, senecios, tiny yellow monkeyflowers, corn lilies.

Vogelsang High Sierra Camp, highest on the Loop Trail, is at an elevation of 10,160 feet. There is a definite exhilaration here at tree line, an on-top-of-the-world euphoria as though one were endowed with some of the restless freedom of the wind, the strength of the icy crags, the far-ranging vision of the golden eagle wheeling serenely in the limitless blue sky. Many travelers on the Loop Trail feel this Camp to be the climax.

If time is available—and it should be made available—one should walk the mile from the Camp to the summit of Vogelsang Pass, providing the Fletcher Creek trail from Merced Lake was chosen. Shortly after leaving the Camp, the trail climbs gently around the shoulder of Fletcher Peak. In the ledges and small terraces between the huge blocks of rocky talus, where snow melt produces bounteous water, look for the little bells of White Heather (Cassiope mertensiana). This dainty little flower blooms somewhat early in the summer, but some of it will be seen into the first part of August. It is a small, creeping, almost prostrate, evergreen shrub, with ascending branches closely covered by needle-like leaves. At the ends of the branches are the tiny, snow-white flowers, cup-shaped with small red sepals which clasp the cups to form a most pleasing contrast. The blossoms are turned down demurely until they begin to dry, when they raise their little heads. Cassiope is lavish in the number of individual blossoms it produces, sometimes seeming to cover the plants as with a light snow. John Muir was especially fond of the white heather and mentions it eloquently on a number of occasions in his writings. For the hiker in the High Country, few flowers will be associated in memory with the wild places of snow and rocks as intimately as cassiope.

Another charming plant of the boggy areas will be found nearby, the American Laurel (Kalmia polifolia var. microphylla). It, too, is a low, many-branched shrub with paired leaves 1/2 to 1 inch long, the stems not more than 3 to 8 inches tall. The handsome rose-colored flowers are cupped discs, about 1/2 inch wide. A unique feature of the blossoms is in the arrangement of the 10 stamens, whose slender filaments, like tiny springs, are tucked into small pouches in the petals until released by the touch of a visiting insect or other sudden motion, thus scattering the pollen. Close examination of any group of flowers will reveal several in either stage.

About halfway to the Pass, situated in a basin directly beneath it, is Vogelsang Lake. The meadow surrounding it is rich in the flora of this high region. Brilliant magenta paintbrush, pale lavender asters, richly purple whorled penstemons, shiny yellow buttercups, brick-red mountain heather—sometimes occurring in startling contrast to the white heather, delicate lemon-yellow monkeyflowers, combine in scatter rugs of colorful designs. The rich carpet of grass encourages the hiker to tarry a while in this sky parlor, to lie down in it, to examine the little flowers face to face. Such a maneuver enables him to make some fascinating discoveries.

For instance, we find the Elephant Heads (Pedicularis groenlandica), richly pink shafts of color 1 to 2 feet tall, rising out of a mass of basal leaves, finely-toothed and almost fern-like. Until you look quite closely, you are not likely to notice the unusual structure of the individual flower in these tall racemes, which give to the plant its appropriate name. Each tiny blossom, about 1/2 inch long, is the miniature head of an elephant—the broad forehead, two large, floppy ears and the upthrust trunk as though it were reaching for a peanut. This flower, and a smaller relative (P. attollens), are widespread in boggy, meadowy areas up to 12,000 feet. Here is your chance actually to see pink elephants!

Above the Lake, on the granite slopes sweeping upward to the Pass, you will notice a vivid rose-purple tone among the gleaming white rocks of the talus. This is a smaller relative of the fireweed, appropriately named Rock-Fringe (Epilobium obcordatum). Growing on short stems, 2 to 6 inches high, it nestles among rocks, seeming to prefer areas of relatively little natural humus. The blossom has 4 petals, each deeply notched, forming a rounded flower about an inch across. This exquisite little bloom seems particularly lovely in this region of harsh rock—another treasured memory of the High Country.

In this high meadow and near the Pass itself, look for the Alpine Willow (Salix anglorum var. antiplasti), a true willow in fact but so tiny as to become a mere part of the ground cover. Its branches creep along the surface, forming mats of willow-like leaves, 3/4 to 1 1/2 inches long. The catkins rise on short stalks, up to 3 inches high, dispensing their woolly seeds as little masses of gray fluff on the meadow grass. This little plant is reasonably common from 9,500 to 12,000 feet.

The Vogelsang area is indeed a sort of alpine climax. Long to be remembered are the moving splendor of the view from the Pass itself; the impressive bulk of Vogelsang Peak (11,516 feet) as seen from the Camp; the idyllic basin of Townsley Lake and the smaller, un-named lakes above it; the vast upland of flower-strewn meadows, known as the Indian Trading Mesa, just north of Townsley Lake; the serrated ranks of peaks marching southeast to join the Sierran crest at the Mt. Lyell axis.

Reluctantly, once again, we leave this region of mountain grandeur to take the trail back to Tuolumne Meadows. As is true wherever we are in Yosemite's High Country, though, we continue to walk through beauty. About a mile from Vogelsang Camp, we cross the flat, rock-strewn expanse of Tuolumne Pass. Much sky-blue lupine is enjoyed through this area, interspersed with yellow senecio, red mountain heather, purple whorled penstemons and others of the grand company of wildflowers we have travelled with on the trail.

In the rocky crevices along the trail look for the Mountain Sorrel (Oxyria digyna), a plant 3 to 12 inches high with rounded, kidney-shaped leaves arranged as a base. From these arise the flower stalks bearing thick clusters of tiny, greenish-yellow to red blooms. The long leaf stalks have a pleasantly acid taste. One of the admirable features of this sorrel is its choice of location, for its grows in dramatically rugged settings in which its almost frail appearance seems emphasized.

From Tuolumne Pass, our trail drops through forests of lodgepole pines to occasional meadow glades, past Rafferty and Johnson Peaks, following Rafferty Creek. In early summer, this is a robust stream, but by mid-August it loses much of its volume. The snow-white blossoms of Labrador-Tea are a frequent sight along the Creek's damp banks, with tall stalks of magenta fireweed adding rich color in late summer. Occasional small tributary streams cross our trail, rising under the high ridges to the west; one in particular is an excellent place to find the dainty little primrose monkeyflower. The tiny bells of white heather decorate stream-side gardens in early summer, before coming into bloom at higher elevations. Toward evening, bird songs permeate the forest, distant music akin to the soft quality of the long rays of golden sunlight slanting through the trees. One of the most memorable is that of the hermit thrush, an ethereal, flute-like series of notes, usually repeated in a more minor key, and seeming to come from far away. Closer at hand, the soft little songs of the juncos are like quiet conversations.

In damp, meadowy areas or stream-sides, we are almost certain to find the tall stalks of Button Parsley, or White Heads *(Sphenosciadium capitellatum)*. The flowers are white, sometimes purplish, and extremely minute but are clustered in dense, hairy balls $1/2$ inch wide. These form in umbels (umbrella-like heads) of 10 to 20 little balls, on stalks $1^1/2$ to 5 feet tall. The long leaves are finely divided into many leaflets, in the manner of carrots, to which family this plant is related. Button parsley is a common trail-side companion at this elevation.

Within a mile and a half of Tuolumne Meadows Lodge, the trail along Rafferty Creek reaches its junction with the John Muir Trail which has come down the adjacent canyon of the Lyell Fork of the Tuolumne River. The forest here is open and sunny, many tall lavender asters waving gently in the mixed sunlight and shadow of these glades. Along the creek and the river Swamp Onions *(Allium validum)* are often seen, with tall stems and rosy-hued flowering heads. The actual blossoms are very small, about $1/2$ inch long, crowded into dense, compact heads $1^1/2$ inches across. The stems rise $1^1/2$ to 3 feet high, and are surrounded by 3 to 6 long leaves, grass-like, rising from the base. There can be no doubt at all that these are onions, for the odor of the leaves is onion-like, with considerable strength. The plant was a favored one with the Indians and early settlers in the Sierra, as it gave zest to their otherwise tasteless diet. They used the bulb as well, but it is hoped that today's Park visitors will refrain from digging them! About a dozen different onion species occur in Yosemite National Park; this is the largest one, found extensively in damp places between 7,000 and 11,000 feet.

As we come back once more into the open reaches of Tuolumne Meadows, we find many of our flower friends following us. Lupines, senecios, larkspurs, whorled penstemons, pussytoes, yampah, short-stemmed goldenrods, dwarf bilberry are present in abundance. Selected areas of good moisture show stands of Western Blue Flag *(Iris missouriensis)*, a very beautiful plant occurring in moist flats and meadows between 3,000 and 11,000 feet. On flower stems 8 to 20 inches high, the 3- to 4-inch wide blossoms have pale blue to lavender stripings. Slender, grass-like leaves rise almost as high as the stems. A typical location is in the meadow just east of the bridge crossing of the Tuolumne.

In late August, two little gentians decorate the short-grass meadows of the High Country, typically Tuolumne and Dana Meadows. The more commonly seen one is the Sierra Gentian *(Gentiana holopetala)*, a short-stemmed (3 to 12 inches), dark-blue to purple tubular flower, 1 to 2 inches long. The flower tube is 4-petalled, each one recurving slightly at the apex. Each stem bears a single erect bloom, held aloft from a base of small pointed leaves $1/2$ to $1^1/2$ inches long. Often the entire plant, flowers and all, seems almost concealed in the grass and sedges of these lush meadows, so that lying prone on the turf is by far the best way to get to know them well.

The other gentian is *Gentiana newberryi*, often called the Alpine Gentian. It is readily distinguished from the purple *G. holopetala* by its white color and the funnel-form tube of the blossom itself. This tube has dark bands on the outside, while the greenish-white interior is speckled with tiny dots. Each stem bears but one flower and is 2 to 4 inches high; the blossom is not more than 2 inches long. As with the Sierra gentian, the stem arises from mostly basal leaves, a bit broader and longer, however. The flowers tend to open only in the afternoon, so that an inspection of a meadow in the morning may yield no results even though they are there for you to admire later. This white gentian is not common in Tuolumne Meadows, but can usually be seen in the Dana Meadows near Tioga Pass Entrance Station.

The High Sierra Loop Trail is indeed the perfect introduction to Yosemite's subalpine zone and its world of wildflowers. More than just a superb botanical garden, this region reveals itself as an aesthetic experience which will always remain in memory as one of life's highlights.

Mary Tresidder, whose entire life was so closely interwoven with Yosemite's beauty, felt it keenly and had the gift for expressing it warmly. Of a camping trip into the headwaters of the Merced River, above Merced Lake High Sierra Camp, she wrote: "I slept in the most beautiful of beds for one of the loveliest of nights. High on the Merced Peak Fork, a crystal stream of the High Sierra, my sleeping bag was cradled in the circling roots of a lodgepole pine and a mountain hemlock, their bases and a few low branches sheltering me from the night wind down the canyon, whose floor fell away in front of me. Far down beyond its mouth rose the peaks at the headwaters of the Merced's Lyell Fork—Lyell and Rodgers and Electra. The sky was full of stars, with the hemlock foliage soft above me. I could scarcely sleep for looking up through it. Then came a saffron dawn, and the form of things became distinct again. I moan that I shall not always remember it in every detail, but I hope I may pass that way again."

And so do we all!

Lemmon's Paintbrush

Meadow Aster

Buttercup

Deer's Tongue

Labrador-Tea

Whorled Penstemon

Arnica

Mountain Daisy

Spiraea

Shieldleaf

Red or Mountain Heather

Dwarf Bilberry

Meadow Monkeyflower

Lobb's Buckwheat

Mountain Pennyroyal

Wallflower

Mule-Ears

Cinquefoil

Mariposa Lily

Lupine

White Heather

American Laurel

Rock-Fringe

Elephant Heads

Mountain Sorrel

Button Parsley

Swamp Onion

Iris

Sierra Gentian

Alpine Gentian

Alpine Willow

Alpine Paintbrush

69

TREE LINE AND ABOVE

When one stands at the high, windy crest of Tioga Pass's 9,941-foot summit, it is easy to believe that the upper limit of vegetation has been reached. True, the White Bark Pines *(Pinus albicaulis)* which are here replacing the lodgepoles and hemlocks, will struggle up another thousand feet on the surrounding peaks until they lie prostrate on the rocky slopes, flattened and sculptured by the buffeting wind of the summits. But surely nothing as delicate as wildflowers could grow in this seeming wasteland of rock—a region where winter lasts from September to mid-July and where a killing frost can occur at any time. And yet they do! In the area above treeline, generally referred to as the alpine zone, about 170 different species of flowers, grasses and sedges have been identified.

One of the most rewarding of alpine rock gardens is the great peak of Mt. Dana (13,053 feet) which rises immediately east of Tioga Pass, just across the open expanse of Dana Meadows. Few areas anywhere can surpass its display of high-elevation flowers, from the lush fields of deep blue lupine at its base to the amazing stands of sky pilot on its lofty summit. In between occurs a rich panorama of other genera which come into bloom in succession from early July to the middle of August and which can provide for the flower enthusiast a rare day of discovery on the westerly slopes of this one mountain.

A trail of sorts from the Tioga Entrance Station leads directly toward the peak itself, passing several idyllic tiny lakes nestled into lawn-like meadows brightened by red heather, yellow potentilla, lavender asters, short-stemmed goldenrod. Approaching the mountain slopes, our little trail strikes boldly upward, climbing determinedly above the broad sweep of meadowy landscape which lies on either side of the Pass.

Here, at the start of our climb, we walk through masses of flowers which, in

Meadow Asters and Mt. Dana

years of generous moisture, provide one of the outstanding displays of the entire Park. Tall Blue Lupines *(Lupinus latifolius* var. *columbianus)* vie with even taller stalks (5 to 6 feet) of dark Purple Larkspur *(Delphinium glaucum)*. The sky blue of Forget-Me-Not *(Hackelia jessicae)* blends in beautifully. All these cool colors are offset by the vivid red of tall Indian Paintbrush *(Castilleja miniata)* and the bright yellow of Arrowhead Groundsel *(Senecio triangularis)*. We have enjoyed these flowers before, but seldom if ever in such dramatically massed effects. This area usually achieves its peak of bloom about the last week of July and the first week of August.

As we climb higher, the trees become fewer and we reach the first of the open, gravelly slopes which mark the definite transition known as tree line. About here, in the first week or two of July, appear the earliest of the mountain's floral displays— before the lush gardens of the lower slopes come into bloom. Certain to be noticed are the low, circular mats of Spreading Phlox *(Phlox diffusa)*, with their 5-petalled blossoms in shades of pink, lavender or white, which we have seen before around Yosemite Valley's rims.

Not so likely to be seen, however, is one of the most amazing of all the Park's flowers—the tiny Steer's Head *(Dicentra uniflora)*. This relative of the bleeding heart of Yosemite Valley grows on a short stem, 2 inches high, with a single pale pink blossom only $1/2$ to $3/4$ inch long. This blossom is an amazingly precise caricature of the bleached skull of a steer—the long snout, empty socket eyes and up-curving horns creating a lasting impression. Nearby are one to three basal leaves dissected into many small lobes, lying flat on the ground. The flower is so small it is very hard to see from normal eye level and may require careful searching. However, once found, the thrill of discovery is ample reward for the effort. Look for it in fine gravel near melting

71

snow banks which keep the area moist. They are in bloom only a week or so, but may be seen in a number of places in the Park between 6,000 and 10,500 feet, when conditions are exactly right—such as near the Upper Gaylor Lake and on Illilouette Ridge's western slope.

The trail to the summit climbs across beautiful grassy meadows, tilted at an angle which produces miniature waterfalls in the small streams singing their way through them. Above these, we reach a rocky plateau where alpine gravel gardens are at their best, normally about the end of July.

In crevices among those rocks, look for stands of the White or Alpine Columbine *(Aquilegia pubescens)* on straight stems 8 to 18 inches high, with several blossoms at the tips. Each petal ends in the typical spur, a repository for the nectar which makes these flowers great favorites of hummingbirds, sphinx moths and large bumble bees with long tongues. This species hybridizes readily with *A. formosa*, of the lower elevations, so we occasionally find tones of cream to yellow to pink to lavender among the white. Unlike its lower elevation relative, though, this columbine carries its flower heads erect on the stems rather than in a drooping posture. One of the most prolific areas in which to find it is the talus slope under the Lying Head, on Mt. Dana.

As we cross the plateau, we are made aware of the predominantly low profile of the plants growing there. All have contrived the rather typical shapes of dense mounds of leaves or low mat-like herbage which enable them to survive the extremely low winter temperatures by burying themselves under thermal blankets of snow. Their low forms also present the least possible surface to the severe winds of the high places, thus lessening the drying effect of this continual turbulence.

One of the more spectacular of these plants is the Alpine Penstemon *(Penstemon davidsonii)*, a memorable purple-violet flower with an inch-long tubular form. It occurs in masses of blooms from a creeping mat of dark-green, small, round leaves and is found commonly between 9,000 and 12,000 feet. Preferring rocky, gravelly locations, it often snuggles against the leeside of an outcrop which gives added protection from wind. This plant blooms almost all summer, from the period soon after the snow banks are gone until the first winter snows begin, perhaps in September.

Another delightful blossom, its bright colors adding to the brilliance of the region, is the Alpine Buckwheat *(Eriogonum ovalifolium* var. *nivale)*. These plants are of the type frequently known as "pincushion plants," and the allusion is obvious. From rounded mounds of silvery-white leaves, so firm they resist even the imprint of a carelessly placed hiking boot, the bright little yellow or rose-colored blooms rise on short stems like decorative pins thrust into an old-fashioned pincushion. The flowers are actually about 1/8 inch long, closely packed into spherical heads some 3/4 inch across. The compact form of the plant is reinforced by a densely woody structure of branches, making it well suited to live for many years in the severe climate of the alpine zone. You will find it a frequent companion on climbs into Yosemite's summits, well above tree line.

The so-called daisies are represented here in this land of the sky, too. Frequently seen in this plateau region on Mt. Dana and in other comparable sites is the Alpine Daisy or Fleabane *(Erigeron compositus* var. *glabratus)*. A dwarf, cushiony plant with a mass of fan-like, hairy, multi-lobed leaves, the short stems rise 2 to 6 inches, with a single blossom on each. The flower is in the traditional form of a daisy—white rays surrounding a yellow center—and is only about an inch in width. An arrangement of these delicate little blossoms on the granite gravels of a lofty alpine garden will be remembered and cherished as an example of nature's utmost care with even the smallest of her creations. In the same general area, you may expect to find a diminutive lupine with pale lilac to white flowers on stems 2 to 4 inches high (*Lupinus lyalli* var. *danaus*). This is Dana's Lupine, named for Mt. Dana, which in turn was named for the eminent American geologist, James Dwight Dana.

Now our trail heads for the 13,000-foot summit of the peak itself. As we leave the plateau and climb over the colorful slabs which make up the mountain's topmost 1,000 feet, we follow occasional splotches of yellow paint across the rocks. No real trail penetrates these heights, and the thin air makes it necessary to proceed slowly. There are advantages in such a slow pace, though, for there is much to see. Mt. Dana raises its lofty crown well above its neighbors; it is the most northerly peak exceeding 13,000 feet in all the Sierra.

Along this last part of our climb, and especially on the summit, the view unfolds in every direction. Mono Lake, to the east, lies almost 6,500 feet below and 10 miles distant, a circular azure mirror reflecting the clouds, like a piece of the sky itself in a setting of silvery-gray ridges. Directly beneath us, the Dana Glacier sprawls across the end of Glacier Canyon, its moraines cradling the turquoise water of Dana Lake, almost 2,000 feet below. To the south rise the twin summits of Mts. Lyell and McClure, their glaciers gleaming in the sunlight. Westward, the long expanses of the Dana and Tuolumne Meadows roll away from our feet to merge with the far away domes and peaks of the area near Lake Tenaya. Our view to the north comprises a bewildering array of crests and valleys, brick-colored with the metamorphic rocks of this part of the Sierra. Saddlebag Lake makes a focal point of interest in the middle of a landscape which extends to the mountain summits at the northernmost boundary of Yosemite National Park.

Not far below the summit we see the first blossoms of a plant which is characteristic of the rocky peaks above tree line. Alpine Gold (*Hulsea algida*), it is named. First collected here on the slopes of Mt. Dana in 1865, it may also be found on many Sierran summits between 10,000 and 13,000 feet. It looks somewhat like an oversized dandelion, producing a brilliant yellow blossom some 2 inches across, one flower at the end of each stem which may rise 4 to 16 inches. The leaves are long and slender and are sharply toothed, rising from the base of the stalks. These stalks, and the flower heads, are sticky and exude a pungent odor resembling balsam. Far above tree line, in the rusty tones of the metamorphic rocks which comprise much of the peak of Mt. Dana, these bright yellow orbs are a visual delight. They form a spectacular color contrast to the vivid red, orange and gold of the lichens which flourish on the rocks of these elevations—rocks which often form landscaped walls surrounding the tiny plots of humus for the hulsea gardens.

Mt. Dana reserves its most remarkable floral treasure for the last. Only those who, like pilgrims seeking a remote shrine, trudge all the way to the top are privileged to behold the Sky Pilot (*Polemonium eximium*). The common name comes from the slang term for one who leads others to heaven; appropriately, it was given to a plant which is found only on or near the tops of the highest peaks. Its pale blue-lavender blossoms, 5-petalled, are crowded together in compact heads, 2 to 3 inches wide, at the tops of stems rising 4 to 12 inches. The leaves appear as small green cylinders and are divided into many tiny leaflets, 3- to 5-parted. The entire plant is somewhat sticky, exuding a sweet, musky odor which seems to pervade the general area. Not the least remarkable characteristic of the polemonium is its ability to flourish in crevices of the summit rocks which appear to offer almost nothing in the way of viable soil. Yet flourish it does in its sky garden, a glorious reward for the weary climber as he stands at last on the mountain top. Polemonium is appropriate to its setting; it is a creature of the sky, the drifting clouds and the summit wind.

While Mt. Dana offers a comprehensive course in the flora of the alpine zone, there are several other flowers of borderline occurrence (i.e., growing just at or immediately below tree line) which are of interest too and should be included here. An especially likely area to look for them is near the little ghost town of Bennettville, a mile north of the highway as it skirts Tioga Lake just east of Tioga Pass. A remnant of the original Tioga Road leads to the town site which consists today of but two wooden buildings, quietly slumbering to the music of a mountain stream. Along this stream, rising from some small lakes another mile north, and in the lush meadow below the town site, rich flower gardens bloom under the bright sunshine—and occasional showers—of late July and August. Many of these flowers we have encountered before, or we have met closely related species. There are several, however, which are new to us and deserve special comment.

Perhaps the most showy of these is the Alpine Monkeyflower (Mimulus tilingii). At the stream margins especially, but wherever there is assured wetness, this brilliantly yellow little flower appears in masses. As with all monkeyflowers, its little face, about an inch across, has the unique form which suggests such a name, the lower lip drooping with heavy jowls. The flower's throat is almost closed by two brown-spotted, or "freckled" ridges. Beneath the mass of yellow blooms is a lush backdrop of bright green, inch-long leaves. This little plant thrives in and near icy streams, forming colorful mats among the warm-toned rocks of the banks. There is a particularly showy colony near the opening of the mine tunnel west of the town site, where a stream of ice water gushes continuously from the tunnel's mouth.

The old, historic road which serves as the trail to Bennettville is a likely place to look for an attractive member of the stonecrop genus, Western Roseroot (Sedum rosea ssp. integrifolium). It clambers over rocks where moisture collects from higher slopes, sometimes forming fringes across the margins of ledges. On stems 2 to 8 inches high, tightly clustered small red flowers make rosettes of bright color. The offsetting green of the small leaves, which are thickly distributed along the stems, is a pleasing color contrast. While the tiny flowers are still in bud, surrounded by the green calyx-lobes, the effect is especially charming—like "caviar in a green jade bowl," Mary Tresidder described it. Roseroot is a flower of early summer—late June or early July—in the High Country. If you look carefully you will find it often, seemingly enjoying the matchless scenery of its homeland from a sunny, rocky eminence.

If one wanders along the stream (Mine Creek) above the town site of Bennettville, there is a good chance of meeting in late August one of the most delicately beautiful of residents of the High Country, Grass of Parnassus (Parnassia palustris var. californica). On slender, grass-like stems, 6 to 15 inches high, the lovely, cream-colored blossoms are borne singly. The 5 petals have prominent green veins and are smooth-edged; the entire blossom is an inch or more across. At the base of the thin stem is a tuft of heart-shaped leaves, an inch long, on extended petioles or stalks. It favors wet areas and can most frequently be found along the margins of streams, though nowhere in abundance. The whole plant presents an elegant aspect, fittingly created to grace the landscape of Mt. Parnassus, mythological home of the god Apollo.

Other flowers demand our attention as we wander through the High Country landscape on a dreamy summer's day, and they too will linger in the memory of such an experience. There will be the Shrubby Cinquefoil (*Potentilla fruticosa*), with brightly yellow flowers, like single roses, decorating generously a low bush of many branches and masses of tiny, needle-like leaves. Tall stalks of Valerian (*Valeriana capitata* var. *californica*), its small white flowers clustered into heads 2 inches wide, seek out areas of early moisture. Delicate little Campion, or Catchfly (*Silene sargentii*), produces small white tubular blossoms with flared petals, preferring rocky crevices. If you look closely in damp, shady areas near rock walls, you may be fortunate enough to see the strange little Mitrewort (*Mitella breweri*), on slender stems from round basal leaves, with tiny green petals divided into a needle-like geometrical design. Many of our old friends from the subalpine zone are present too—scarlet paint-brush, pink asters, purple whorled penstemons, golden tones of senecio and wall-flower, white heather, the brick-red of bryanthus (red heather), tall, white button parsley, orange-toned columbines, magenta mountain-pride, pink elephant heads, lavender wild onions, lupines in assorted shades of blue and violet. And more, many, many more! Early August is the moment of truth for the floral regions at tree line and above. The business of blooming and then setting their seeds must be attended to promptly, for the days are dropping away like autumn leaves and winter can begin in September. So the urge to bloom is seen everywhere, with magnificent results!

Here, then, is the last act in the drama of spring's pilgrimage from the foothills, which began in March. For six months we have been privileged to observe her progress up the mountain slopes of the Sierra, across the canyons and meadows and ridges of Yosemite. Appropriately, she rings down the curtain for this year with a spectacular show of color and form and diversity of species, displayed on a stage of unparalleled grandeur among the peaks and high glacial basins.

Though we may have regrets when September turns the meadows to gold and the tiny leaves of the dwarf bilberry flame in the grass, there is deep satisfaction in knowing that the magnificent production will be re-staged next year. Anyone fortunate enough to see at least some of spring's performance can breathe a little prayer with Mary Tresidder, "I hope I may pass that way again."

Steer's Head

Alpine Penstemon

Alpine Buckwheat

Alpine Columbine

Alpine Daisy

Alpine Gold

Sky Pilot

Alpine Monkeyflower

Western Roseroot

Shrubby Cinquefoil

Grass of Parnassus

Campion or Catchfly

INDEX

PLANT NAMES, TEXT REFERENCES AND ILLUSTRATIONS

Common names, printed in Roman letters, are arranged alphabetically among botanical names, which are shown in italics. The appropriate botanical name is also shown in parentheses following the common name, and vice versa.

Each flower name is followed by one or more numbers: those in bold face indicate the page numbers of illustrations, those in light face the text reference pages. For example:

Tidy Tips *(Layia fremontii)*, 8, 12, **13**

If there is no bold face numeral, the plant is not illustrated.

Deer Brush *(Ceanothus integerrimus)*, 29, 36, 41, **42**
Deer's Tongue *(Frasera speciosa)*, 37, 50, **64**
Delphinium glaucum (Larkspur, Purple), 52, 53, 58, 62, 71
Delphinium hansenii (Larkspur), 12
Delphinium nuttallianum (Larkspur), 33, 38, **44**
Dicentra chrysantha (Golden Ear-Drops), 19
Dicentra formosa (Bleeding Heart), 19, **25, 71**
Dicentra uniflora (Steer's Head), 19, 71, **76**
Dodecatheon jeffreyi (Shooting Star), 31, 36, **43,** 51, 54, 58
Dodecatheon jeffreyi ssp. *pygmaeum* (Shooting Star, Pigmy), 50
Dodecatheon hansenii (Shooting Star, Dwarf), 12
Dogbane *(Apocynum pumilum)*, 35
Dogwood, American *(Cornus stolonifera)*, 16, 38, 39, 40, **47**
Dogwood, Creek *(Cornus stolonifera)*, 16, 38, 39, 40, **47**
Dogwood, Mountain *(Cornus nuttallii)*, 17, **24**
Dogwood, Red Osier *(Cornus stolonifera)*, 16, 38, 39, 40, **47**
Dudleya cymosa (Stonecrop), 12, **15**
Elderberry *(Sambucus caerulea)*, 23
Elderberry, Red *(Sambucus microbotrys)*, 35
Elephant Heads *(Pedicularis groenlandica)*, 60, **68,** 75
Elephant Heads, Little *(Pedicularis attollens)*, 61
Epilobium angustifolium (Fireweed), 34, **44,** 61
Epilobium obcordatum (Rock-Fringe), 61, **68**
Erigeron compositus var. *glabratus* (Daisy, Alpine), 72, **76**
Erigeron peregrinus (Daisy, Mountain), 52, **65**
Eriodictyon californicum (Yerba Santa), 23
Eriogonum lobbii (Buckwheat, Lobb's), 56, **66**
Eriogonum ovalifolium var. *nivale* (Buckwheat, Alpine), 72, **76**
Eriogonum umbellatum (Sulphur Flower), 34, 36, **45,** 55, 57, 58
Erysimum capitatum (Wallflower), 35
Erysimum perenne (Wallflower), 55, 60, **66,** 75
Eschscholzia californica (Poppy, California), 11, **14**
Fairy Lantern *(Calochortus albus)*, 9, **13**
Farewell-to-Spring *(Clarkia purpurea* ssp. *quadrivulnera)*, 10
Fiddleneck *(Amsinckia intermedia* var. *eastwoodae)*, 12
Fir, Red *(Abies magnifica)*, 36, 39, 40
Fir, White *(Abies concolor)*, 41
Fireweed *(Epilobium angustifolium)*, 34, **44,** 61
Five-Spot *(Nemophila maculata)*, 12, **15**
Flag, Western Blue *(Iris missouriensis)*, 62, **69**
Flannel-Bush *(Fremontia californica)*, 12, **15**
Fleabane *(Erigeron compositus* var. *glabratus)*, 72, **76**
Forget-Me-Not, Alpine *(Hackelia jessicae)*, 71
Forget-Me-Not, Sierra *(Hackelia velutina)*, 34, 35, **45,** 53, 57, 58, 60
Frasera speciosa (Deer's Tongue), 37, 50, **64**
Fremontia californica (Flannel-Bush), 12, **15**
Fresno Mat *(Ceanothus fresnensis)*, 30
Fritillaria pinetorum (Fritillary, Davidson's), 34, **45**
Fritillary, Davidson's *(Fritillaria pinetorum)*, 34, **45**
Fuschia, California *(Zauschneria californica* ssp. *latifolia)*, 35, **45**
Gentian, Alpine *(Gentiana newberryi)*, 63, **69**

Gentian, Green *(Frasera speciosa)*, 37, 51, **64**
Gentian, Sierra *(Gentiana holopetala)*, 62, 63, **69**
Gentiana holopetala (Gentian, Sierra), 62, 63, **69**
Gentiana newberryi (Gentian, Alpine), 63, **69**
Geranium richardsonii (Geranium, Wild), 37, **47**
Geranium, Wild *(Geranium richardsonii)*, 37, **47**
Gilia, Scarlet *(Ipomopsis aggregata)*, 39, **46**
Ginger, Wild *(Asarum hartwegii)*, 19, **25**
Godetia *(Clarkia dudleyana)*, 10, **13**, 21
        (Clarkia purpurea ssp. *quadrivulnera)*, 10
Golden Ear-Drops *(Dicentra chrysantha)*, 19
Golden Stars *(Brodiaea gracilis)*, 52, 54
        (Brodiaea lutea var. *scabra)*, 9, 12, **13**, 37
Goldenrod, Meadow *(Solidago canadensis* ssp. *elongata)*, 23, **27**, 51, 56, 57, 62, 70
Goldfields *(Baeria chrysostoma)*, 8
Gooseberry *(Ribes montigenum)*, 58
Grass Nuts *(Brodiaea pulchella)*, 12
Grass of Parnassus *(Parnassia palustris* var. *californica)*, 74, **77**
Groundsel, Arrowhead *(Senecio triangularis)*, 33, 36, 37, 38, 40, **44**, 52, 53, 55, 56, 57,
    58, 60, 61, 62, 71, 75
Habenaria dilatata var. *leucostachys* (Orchid, Sierra Rein), 31, **43**
Hackelia jessicae (Forget-Me-Not, Alpine), 71
Hackelia velutina (Forget-Me-Not, Sierra), 34, 35, **45**, 53, 57, 58, 60
Heather, Mountain *(Phyllodoce breweri)*, 54, 55, 56, 57, 60, 61, **65**, 70, 75
Heather, Red *(Phyllodoce breweri)*, 54, 55, 56, 57, 60, 61, **65**, 70, 75
Heather, White *(Cassiope mertensiana)*, 60, 62, **67**, 75
Helenium bigelovii (Sneezeweed), 20, **26**
Helianthus annuus (Sunflower), 20
Hellebore, False *(Veratrum californicum)*, 32, 38, **43**, 53, 55, 58, 60
Hemlock, Mountain *(Tsuga mertensiana)*, 53, 55
Heracleum lanatum (Cow Parsnip), **17**, 20, **25**, 58
Heuchera micrantha var. *erubescens* (Alum-Root), 30, **42**
Holodiscus boursieri (Cream Bush), 37, **47**
Hulsea algida (Alpine Gold), 73, **76**
Hypericum formosum var. *scouleri* (St. Johns Wort), 21, **26**
Hyssop, Giant *(Agastache urticifolia)*, 23, **27**
Ipomopsis aggregata (Gilia, Scarlet), 39, **46**
Iris *(Iris hartwegii)*, 35
Iris hartwegii (Iris), 35
Iris missouriensis (Flag, Western Blue), 62, **69**
Ivesia santolinoides (Mousetails), 37, 51
Kalmia polifolia var. *microphylla* (Laurel, American), 60, **67**
Knotweed *(Polygonum bistortoides)*, 35, **47**
Labrador-Tea *(Ledum glandulosum* var. *californicum)*, 51, 53, 54, 56, 61, **64**
Languid Lady *(Mertensia ciliata* var. *stomatechoides)*, 32, 38, **43**
Larkspur *(Delphinium hansenii)*, 12
        (Delphinium nuttallianum), 33, 38, **44**
Larkspur, Purple *(Delphinium glaucum)*, 52, 53, 58, 62, 71
Laurel, American *(Kalmia polifolia* var. *microphylla)*, 60, **67**
Layia fremontii (Tidy Tips), 8, 12, **13**
Ledum glandulosum var. *californicum* (Labrador-Tea), 51, 53, 54, 56, 61, **64**

Pipsissewa *(Chimaphila umbellata* var. *occidentalis)*, 20, **26**
Plagiobothrys nothofulvus (Popcorn Flower), 12
Platystemon californicus (Cream Cup), 12
Polemonium eximium (Sky Pilot), 70, 73, **77**
Polygonum bistortoides (Knotweed), 35, **47**
Popcorn Flower *(Plagiobothrys nothofulvus)*, 12
Poppy, California *(Eschscholzia californica)*, 11, **14**
Populus tremuloides (Aspen), 55
Potentilla fruticosa (Cinquefoil, Shrubby), 70, 75, **77**
Potentilla gracilis ssp. *nuttallii* (Cinquefoil), 59, **67**
Primrose, Evening *(Oenothera hookeri)*, 22, **27**
Prince's Pine *(Chimaphila umbellata* var. *occidentalis)*, 20, **26**
Prunus emarginata (Cherry, Bitter), 35
Pterospora andromedea (Pinedrop), 18, **24**
Pussy Paws *(Calyptridium umbellatum)*, 19, **25**, 37, 54, 56, 57, 58, 60
Pussytoes *(Antennaria rosea)*, 51, 52, 55, 62
Pyrola picta (Shinleaf, White-Veined), 38, **46**
Quercus kelloggii (Oak, Black), 16, 41
Quercus vaccinifolia (Oak, Huckleberry), 41
Ranunculus alismaefolius var. *alismellus* (Buttercup), 50, 53, 55, 57, 60, **64**
Redbud, Western *(Cercis occidentalis)*, 10, **14**
Rhododendron occidentale (Azalea, Western), **17,** 18, **24,** 41, 58
Ribes montigenum (Gooseberry), 58
Ribes nevadense (Currant, Sierra), 35
Rock-Fringe *(Epilobium obcordatum)*, 61, **68**
Roseroot, Western *(Sedum rosea* ssp. *integrifolium)*, 74, **77**
Rudbeckia californica (Coneflower, California), 30, **42**
Rudbeckia hirta var. *pulcherrima* (Black-Eyed Susan), 21, **26**
Rubus parviflorus (Thimbleberry), 35, 40, **47**
Rue, Meadow *(Thalictrum fendleri)*, 38, 40, **46**
St. John's Wort *(Hypericum formosum* var. *scouleri)*, 21, **26**
Salix anglorum var. *antiplasti* (Willow, Alpine), 61, **69**
Sambucus caerulea (Elderberry), 23
Sambucus microbotrys (Elderberry, Red), 35
Sandwort *(Arenaria kingii)*, 57
Sarcodes sanguinea (Snow Plant), 18, **24**, 36, 40
Sedum obtusatum (Stonecrop), 40, 52
Sedum rosea ssp. *integrifolium* (Roseroot, Western), 74, **77**
Senecio triangularis (Groundsel, Arrowhead), 33, 36, 37, 38, 40, **44,** 52, 53, 55, 56, 57, 58,
      60, 61, 62, 71, 75
Sequoiadendron giganteum (Big Tree), 28
Service-Berry *(Amelanchier pallida)*, 37
Shieldleaf *(Streptanthus tortuosus)*, 23, 35, 37
            (Streptanthus tortuosus var. *orbiculatus)*, 52, 53, 54, 55, **65**
Shinleaf, White-Veined *(Pyrola picta)*, 38, **46**
Shooting Star *(Dodecatheon jeffreyi)*, 31, 36, **43,** 51, 54, 58
Shooting Star, Dwarf *(Dodecatheon hansenii)*, 12
Shooting Star, Pigmy *(Dodecatheon jeffreyi* ssp. *pygmaeum)*, 50
Silene californica (Pink, Indian), 11, **14**
Silene sargentii (Campion), 75, **77**
Sky Pilot *(Polemonium eximium)*, 70, 73, **77**

PLANT HABITAT TEXT REFERENCES